SOME PROBLEMS OF
CATHOLIC HIGHER EDUCATION
IN THE UNITED STATES

SOME PROBLEMS OF

CATHOLIC HIGHER EDUCATION

IN THE UNITED STATES

Roy J. Deferrari, Ph.D.

Professor of Greek and Latin, Emeritus

THE CATHOLIC UNIVERSITY OF AMERICA

ST. PAUL EDITIONS

Library of Congress Catalog Card Number: 63-23364

Copyright, 1963, by the *Daughters of St. Paul*

Printed by the *Daughters of St. Paul*
50 St. Paul's Ave., Jamaica Plain, Boston, Mass. 02130

FOREWORD

It is not often that a pupil has the privilege of preceding his master's narrative with an introduction, but this is the case here, for Roy Deferrari taught me early in my life-work—and well—what every young man, aspiring to a higher education, should know about that portion under Roman Catholic patronage (I still do not pretend to understand all I know). The place of instruction, usually, was the regular semiannual occasion when the Commission on Institutions of Higher Education of the Middle States Association of Colleges and Secondary Schools (fondly known as *The* Commission), convened to do its accrediting business.

As the memorable Yogi Berra of the New York Yankees has sagely remarked," You can observe a lot by watchin'." I and many other members of The Commission are the benefactors of Roy Deferrari's practiced, surgical mind

9

which could quickly dissect the strengths and weaknesses of a college or university and diagnose instanter whether the institution's health would permit it, in the one case, to convalesce on the Association's prestigious membership list, or, in the other, to lick its wounds and linger longingly, sometimes in moribund condition, still in the in-patient department, and he never let compassion become suspended judgment in inoperable cases.

But if Mr. Deferrari has a sharp eye for foreign motes, he never had a dull one for domestic beams, as his writings including this one, testify.

Long before the current fashion began of establishing "dialogues" between disparate groups having related interests, and the advent of the Ecumenical Council II, Roy Deferrari initiated his own colloquy in regional and national educational forums. Few now realize the majestic dimensions of the ignorance of Roman Catholic higher education which characterized the non-Roman Catholic academic community up until 1945-50. This unenlightenment is traceable to two causes: (1) The diffidence of Catholic educators to invite "their separated brethren" (but still "brethren") into their halls of learning coupled with a reluctance to participate in regional and national educational activities open to all, and (2) a tendency on the part of those "brethren" to dismiss Roman Catholic higher education as monolithic and non-intellectual.

The pages which follow draw from the vast reservoir of a half century of experience and observation in higher education. It is written with candor and the trenchant insight of one who has been a direct witness. The book will probably appeal most to various groups of religious struggling with new institutions (or with ideas to found one) and to those operating colleges still immature even after several years of existence.

Many chapters and discussions stand out: Chapter 4 on The Challenge of the Catholic College for Women Today;

the importance of the integration of the curriculum (with Catholic philosophy and purpose); the nature of graduate study; and the conditions of employment for lay faculty, are some.

I do not agree with everything Roy Deferrari espouses. Neither will all Roman Catholic educators. This is another way of saying that the book should be provocative, as are all of Deferrari's writings.

I have different views, for instance, on the dangers of academic inbreeding (here, though, Deferrari eventually appears to agree with me when, in Chapter 14, he advises religious to seek admission for graduate work to the best possible institutions). I would put more emphasis on the importance of recruiting lay faculty and the improvement of their conditions of employment than he does. I would want to make it plainer that at least two agencies exist which have a sophisticated and real understanding of Roman Catholic institutions and their special purposes and objectives (The Commission alluded to earlier and the State Education Department in New York). And, finally, I have some different views about higher institutions operated by religious solely for their own education.

Throughout the book, the author deals, in varying depths, with four problems which peculiarly may jeopardize the educational effectiveness of institutions under Roman Catholic sponsorship (these are summarized well in a recent issue of *America*):

1. The possible pre-eminence of piety and the consequent necessity for vigilance against excessive preoccupation with moral and spiritual excellence which might adumbrate the primacy of an institution's intellectual function.

2. The danger of excessive control and supervision from remote ecclesiastical officials resulting in unreasonable interference with the work in what should be an autonomous institution.

3. The dual nature of the faculty which may sometimes lead to inequitable treatment of the lay portion and double standards in conditions of employment.

4. The traditional exercise of authority in an hierarchical system based on obedience which may result in arbitrary decision-making and disenfranchisement of those affected in an institution which by its very nature must be incurably democratic and should operate through a "dynamic of consensus" in an atmosphere of freedom.

I commend this work not only to those in Roman Catholic colleges and universities but also to those in the academic community who would seek to understand the nature and unique purpose of such institutions. Roy Deferrari knows what excellence is and what can attenuate it. In the immortal words of the historian, Carl Becker, in his knowledge of higher education, the author has few peers and absolutely no equal.

October 29, 1963

EWALD B. NYQUIST

Deputy Commissioner of Education

The University of the State of New York

The State Education Department

INTRODUCTION

This book may well be considered an extension of my "Memoirs of The Catholic University of America, 1918-1960" which appeared in 1961. However, it differs from its predecessor in one very important respect. In the "Memoirs" I was concerned primarily with presenting a record of events during an extensive and important period of the University's development, together with a portrayal of some of the overtones involved. My intention was to place comparatively little emphasis on my personal opinions, which I had hoped would be received as just that and nothing more. Incidentally, I was not as successful as I had hoped to be in this latter respect, in spite of the fact that I had written with reference to my personal views: "If these

13

opinions have no value they can easily be discarded and no harm will be done." The reaction which flared up in several quarters might well be said to have been heated.

In the present volume I deal not so much with individuals and events as with the ideas and policies of higher education, the proper understanding and development of which determine the quality and excellence of any college or university activity, Catholic or non-Catholic. This feature will probably not require my mentioning the name of anyone, although, since I am definitely concerned at all times with The Catholic University of America, especially its college, readers who know even a little about the history of the University will with confidence deduce the identity of the individual or individuals chiefly concerned, and in most instances will be wrong in their deductions. The material of this book emanates chiefly from my experience at The Catholic University of America, especially in the University's work of affiliation, and my contacts with other American institutions of higher education, while in attendance for many years at the annual meetings of the Association of American Universities, of the Middle Altantic States Association of Colleges and Secondary Schools, having served for many years on the Commission on Higher Education of that organization, and of the College and University Section of the National Catholic Educational Association.

In the light of this experience, I feel justified in expressing my personal opinion on certain problems which have beset The Catholic University of America and other similar institutions through the years. Again, I declare that, if these opinions are worthy of no consideration whatsoever, they may easily be ignored. But my earnest hope is that this expression of my ideas will to some degree be of benefit in the future to The Catholic University of America and to all Catholic higher education, to which I have devoted all the energy and effort of a long life.

The various topics discussed in these pages have necessarily been treated in individual chapters. The arrangement of the chapters of this book is confessedly subjective. I have tried to organize them in a manner that will contribute to holding the interest of the reader from the beginning of his examination of the book until the end.

In the United States of America all institutions of higher education obtain the right to operate and to grant degrees through the individual States in which they are located. This involves the granting of an appropriate charter or incorporation to the institution concerned. In this process there is no indication of quality whatsoever. In a few instances, e.g. the States of New York and Pennsylvania, no charter or incorporation is granted unless certain qualitative requirements are met, but, ordinarily, the academic excellence of an institution of higher education is determined by private groups made up of representatives of the institution's peers, e.g. the regional associations and the professional organizations. Thus the ideas and considerations which are set forth in this book are not such as have been fixed by any state or federal group, as would regularly be the case in every other country of the world, but the general views of the leading educators of the land as expressed by them in public meetings and professional publications. Admittedly there may be some differences of opinion among them, but fundamentally they are of one opinion in these matters.

It will not be presumptuous for me to add that this book may be regarded as one of a trilogy. The first, Memoirs of The Catholic University of America, 1918-1960, represents my personal experiences, the second, the present volume, Some Problems of Catholic Higher Education in the United States, is a discussion of some over-all problems of the field; and the third, A Handbook on Administration in Catholic Institutions of Higher Education, soon to appear from the press, consists of some practical recommendations for administrators. All these taken together crystallize and make clear my activities at The Catholic University of America over the years. It may appear that there is some over-lapping between the present volume, Some Problems of Catholic Higher Education in the United States, and the Handbook on Administration. This will appear to be true in several instances, but the treatment of the topics, as will be seen, is quite different: one will be a general discussion of the entire problem involved with its several ramifications; the other will be from the point of view of giving practical information.

It is indeed my wish and prayer that the expression of these opinions as set forth in this trilogy will be of genuine benefit to The Catholic University of America and all Catholic institutions of higher education.

TABLE OF CONTENTS

17

18   *Contents*

Ille veritatis defensor esse debet,

qui quum recte sentit loqui non metuit,

nec erubescit.

I owe this quotation to Professor Eric
Cochrane of the University of Chicago.
It probably is from Saint Ambrose.

CHAPTER ONE

THE ORGANIZATION OF INSTITUTIONS OF HIGHER EDUCATION

The organization of institutions of higher education on the collegiate level for the most part presents few major problems. Most colleges of whatever type are of simple organization and their control by the President and the Board of Trustees should cause little difficulty. It is only when these institutions seek to expand and offer work in the professional fields [1] or in areas not in harmony with a liberal arts program as regularly proclaimed by the College of Arts and Sciences that serious problems arise. By reason of the varying purposes involved difficulties of control by the President and the Board of Trustees present themselves and this is an extremely im-

[1] Chapter Three on the General College and Professional Education.

21

portant matter in Catholic institutions where the importance of a Catholic point of view throughout the college's activity is constantly stressed and must be guarded. Otherwise, the very reason for the existence of the Catholic college disappears.

We have many excellent colleges whose administrators by choice seek to conduct an ever improving college of liberal arts or, as some in this age prefer to call it, a general college, and who deliberately refuse to take on any professional program or similar activity whose chief aim is counter to that of a liberal education. Thus the organization of these colleges remains a simple one, and experience shows that they achieve their main purpose, that of a liberal education, to a highly successful degree. It is, of course, true that a college of liberal arts which takes on a professional program contributes much benefit to this program, but it receives many new problems and probably very few benefits for its own peculiar aims. The fields of professional study usually found in a general college, more or less formally organized, sometimes even as schools, are Nursing, Library Service, Social Work, and even Graduate Work leading to a Master's Degree in a few departments.

It is for the most part agreed that professional studies prosper most when in close contact with general studies. Certainly they must have this influence and not attempt to develop by themselves in a ghetto kind of existence. But the best results are achieved when this development takes place in a well organized university.

The great question, still unanswered, in American academic circles is: "What is a University in America today?" A common definition of a University is "An institution organized for teaching and study in the higher branches of learning and empowered to confer degrees in special departments, as theology, law, medicine, and the arts. In the United States, a university typically comprises a college and one or more graduate or professional schools." [1]

It is not our purpose to discuss this question in any detail here but a few basic facts should be known by everyone interested in the meaning of Catholic higher education in the United States. Any well informed person knows at once what is meant by a university in France, the English universities or a German university, but no one can tell with accuracy what an American university is. The fundamental difficulty lies in the fact that the names "university" and "college" as used in the official titles of institutions are quite worthless as indications of their academic character. Of the many so-called universities in this country, the majority are colleges of varying quality, some no better even than poor high schools. On the other hand we have Bryn Mawr

[1] Webster's New Collegiate Dictionary, s.v.

College which offers genuine university instruction in most of the fields covered by the outstanding universities of the land. The reason for this situation, of course, is clear. All countries which profess to have educational systems, except the United States, have a national educational bureau of some kind which exercises complete control over the country's school system, whereas here in our country the control of education is left to the individual states which with few exceptions, e.g. New York, Pennsylvania, and a few others, are content to leave the supervision in the hands of the educators themselves.

The problem is further complicated by the growing practice of professed colleges offering graduate work in a number of the liberal arts and even a program in the professions, while the declared universities have expanded the undergraduate college to a point where with a tremendous athletic program it completely dominates the entire nature of the institution. As a whole, American universities appear to be trying to do too much all at once, usually with entirely inadequate resources, in particular instructors and endowment. One disastrous result is that the members of the faculty, who are, with the exception of the members of the professional faculties, almost always college teachers, are terribly over-burdened with teaching and administrative duties. The inevitable result of this is that few of them can carry on much serious research, and this is especially true of the Catholic titular universities.

The usual university organization found in Europe includes the four faculties of philosophy (or arts), law, medicine, and theology with the development of scientific studies; especially in recent years, many universities have also added scientific schools or faculties.

Under these circumstances the European conception of a university has been lost in the United States, and it is difficult to see how or when it will be regained. At one time it was clearly seen that, as institutions, the college and the university, having very different purposes, demand a different organization and administration, but pressure from influential sources and local necessities of the hour have made it practically impossible for the university and the college in United States to exist apart. Writing at the turn of the century for the Encyclopedia Americana, Edward Delavan Perry of Columbia University wrote: "There are still but two institutions which may be called even fragmentary universities entirely unconnected with a college: The Clark University of Worcester, Massachusetts, and the Catholic University of America at Washington." As far as The Catholic University of America is concerned this statement at the present time is quite incongruous. The enrollment of undergraduate students is beginning to pass that of graduate students and in many classes it is difficult to determine whether the quality of instruction is geared to one group of students or the other. This situation is probably due to the general tendency here in the United States for the two types of institutions to grow together. The colleges boast of special kinds of curriculums which in their upper two years employ graduate methods of instruction and promote independent study. Furthermore, as we have said, the colleges even offer programs leading to graduate degrees. The universities are offering undergraduate programs; some say primarily to increase the financial income of the institution. Certainly, by social activities and by unreasonably expanded athletic programs, they are doing everything in their power to increase the undergraduate enrollments. Some educators argue in favor of this trend. For obvious reasons I definitely do not. The idea of most of our early founders of a university devoted primarily to graduate studies with undergraduate programs of restricted enrollment slanted toward still higher studies continues to appeal to me most.

Monsignor Edward A. Pace in the Catholic Encylopedia wrote as follows: "Present Law of the Church.–The principal laws now in force regarding universities are as follows: 1. For the establishment of a complete Catholic university, including the faculties of theology and canon law, the authorization of the Pope is necessary; and this alone suffices if the foundation is made with ecclesiastical funds or private endowment. If public funds of the State are also used for the purpose, authorization must likewise be obtained from the civil power. The Church, moreover, recognizes the right of the State to establish purely secular faculties, e.g. of law and medicine. 2. The Church requires that in universities founded by the civil power for Catholics, the faculties of theology and canon law, once they are canonically established, shall remain subject to the supreme ecclesiastical authority, and moreover, that professors in other faculties shall be Catholic, and that their teaching shall accord with Catholic doctrine and moral principles. 3. As appears from recent Papal Charters, the university enjoys autonomy, e.g. in the appointment of instructors, the regulation of studies, and the conferring of degrees in accordance with the Statutes. 4. By the Constitution 'Sapienti Consilio,' 29 June, 1908, the Congregation of Studies is charged with all questions regarding the establishment of new Catholic universities and important changes in those already founded. 5. Degrees in theology and canon law, conferred without examination by the Holy See through the Congregation of Studies, give the recipient the same rights and privileges as the degrees conferred after examination by a Catholic university."

There exists in the United States today the Association of American Universities, as an integral part of which is the Association of Graduate Schools. This professedly is not an accrediting agency, but it cannot be denied that membership in this organization is a strong indication of the existence of a considerable amount of research of high quality therein. In fact, from the very beginning of its establishment the basic criterion of election to membership in this association has been the active progress of genuine research in at least five areas of study. Furthermore, membership in the organization is obtained not by application but by invitation from the officials of the group on the recommendation of a committee on membership. At present there are forty-two members, only one of which, The Catholic University of America, is Catholic. I personally would not say that there are no other Catholic universities that are worthy of becoming members, but I feel that this is an indication of a general weakness in our Catholic universities. Within the last few years a number of Catholic institutions have legally changed their names from that of college to that of university. As far as I can see their chief claim to this change of title lies in an extremely large undergraduate body, several schools in addition to the college, the granting of numerous Master's degrees, and very little activity in the area of the Ph.D. and post-doctoral research. Indeed, the great weakness of our Catholic graduate schools, both new and of long standing, is the low quality of their research activity. There are some reasons for this situation, but expressing them here will not resolve the problem.

The question is sometimes raised: "Can a university best achieve its purposes by an organization consisting of a relatively loose federation of autonomous schools and colleges or by close centralization?" For it appears clear that universities in the United States, whether Catholic or non-Catholic will consist, in spite of all arguments and theories, of an undergraduate college, a graduate school, and one or more professional schools.

It seems to me that this question has but one answer for a Catholic university, and that is an organization of close centralization. Only by such an organization can an administration make sure that the indispensable aims of Catholic education are being achieved and maintained even approximately. It might be added that an organization of close centralization becomes more difficult to maintain as the institution becomes more widespread physically. This is especially true when so-called schools or divisions which have a rather distinct entity in themselves, such as the professional groups, are established at a considerable distance from the administrative center of operation. It then becomes almost natural with these units to develop with very little contact with the institution's source of unification, the central administration. This results not only in the administrative malfunctioning of the university but the probability of the weakening or total disappearance of the special Catholic features of its operations in the face of the school's or division's interest in its own special or professional aims.

Another question of importance arises here. Should a professional or technical school be allowed to expand indefinitely to the point where it completely dominates the entire institution? Obviously, not! By the very nature of things, a strong college of arts and sciences with an accompanying graduate school will keep the proper balance in a complex institution and preserve its aims in a true perspective. The members of the faculties of these two groups will be the guiding forces in this most important function.

The aims of Catholic education are common to all its levels. The general college is not alone responsible for achieving them. Unfortunately they have been saddled upon the general college almost exclusively but, of course, they should be the responsibility of all educational activity under Catholic auspices. They have been very aptly summarized as follows:

"To produce the true and finished man of character, the man who has

Cf. Sister Emanuel Collins, O.S.F., Affiliation Bulletin for Institutions of Higher Education, Series XVIII, No. 1.

(1) The sound knowledge of Catholic theology basic to the formation of the Christian character;

(2) A 'philosophical mind' with habits of intellectual curiosity, discriminating inquiry, and precision;

(3) The ability to speak, read, write, and listen intelligently;

(4) An understanding and appreciation of his cultural heritage;

(5) An understanding of the physical world around him;

(6) Christian principles and attitudes toward man as a social and political being; and,

(7) A sound knowledge and proper habits of physical and mental health."

All of the aims mentioned above are quite appropriate to the Catholic college, but none of them can be completely ignored in any phase of Catholic post-collegiate education, if the term "Catholic" is to have any appreciable significance. The sixth statement above has increasing significance as Catholic education continues in various ramifications.

Whatever policy of expansion and development is adopted by a Catholic institution of higher education, the following are the chief problems which it must face and which will give meaning to the Catholic education which it professes to offer. All these will be treated in the course of this book:

I. The Organization of Institutions of Higher Education.

II. Some Problems of Catholic Higher Education.

III. The Responsibilities of the General College and Professional Education.

IV. The Challenge of the Catholic College for Women Today.

V. The Problem of Research in Catholic Institutions of Higher Education.

VI. The College Curriculum and the Importance of Integration.

VII. Graduate Study in Primarily Undergraduate Institutions.

VIII. Discipline in Catholic Institutions of Higher Education.

IX. Faculty Participation in the Life of an Institution.

X. Bargain Teachers in Catholic Higher Education.

XI. Members of the Clergy and Laity as Teachers and Administrators in Catholic Higher Education.

XII. Catholic Educators and Their Relations with Non-Catholic Educators.

XIII. Catholic Institutions of Higher Education and Public Opinion.

XIV. Problems in Higher Education for Sisters.

XV. The Religious Community College for Women.

XVI. The Catholic Junior College.

XVII. State and Regional Accreditation: Before and After.

XVIII. Cooperation in Catholic Higher Education.

XIX. The Advisability of a Summer Session.

XX. Workshops.

XXI. Adult Education.

XXII. Financing the Education of Students in Catholic Schools.

XXIII. The Future Development of Catholic Higher Education.

XXIV. Final Appraisal of Catholic Higher Education.

CHAPTER TWO

SOME PROBLEMS OF CATHOLIC HIGHER EDUCATION IN THE UNITED STATES.

This book takes its title from the heading of this chapter. While we believe that each chapter of this volume contributes something to the understanding of the problems of Catholic higher education, it will be appropriate to consider this subject briefly as a whole.

In the present generation educators generally have been emphasizing the importance to every institution of higher education of a clear and full statement of its purposes. To the achievement of these purposes all activities of the college or university should contribute something or the activity can not justify its existence. This statement should reflect by its conciseness, its clarity, and the excellence of phraseology, the results of a thorough and comprehensive study of the very reason for that institution's being.

It is also a conviction among educators that the quality of an educational institution can best be attained by determining the success with which it has achieved its purposes. Thus it follows that a small college which does set up limited aims for itself but has accomplished them superlatively well is a better academic institution than a large one which has a wide variety of aims and in spite of the resources available to achieve them has done so very inadequately. All this, of course, involves the nature of the curriculum, admissions process, faculty training, extra-curricular activities, library development, and graduation requirements.

A word of caution might be given with respect to the emphasis on the spiritual objectives of the institution almost to the exclusion of the intellectual objectives. Pope Pius XI, in his encyclical *The Christian Education of Youth,* re-stated the definition of Christian education as follows:

.... Christian education takes in the whole aggregate of human life, physical and spiritual, intellectual and moral, individual, domestic and social, not with a view to reducing it in any way, but in order to elevate, regulate, and perfect it, in accordance with the example and teaching of Christ.

Hence the true Christian, the product of Christian education, is the supernatural man who thinks, judges, and acts constantly and consistently in accordance with the example and teaching of Christ; in other words, to use the current term, the true and finished man of character.

Thus, in presenting the aims and purposes (the meaning) of Catholic higher education, two general approaches must be kept in mind, neither one of which can appropriately be subordinated to the other: (1) the spiritual objectives of the institution should be carefully described as a part of the sum total of the student's religious experience toward achieving his final goal and (2) the specific intellectual purpose should be presented both in general and in particular terms.

It should not cause alarm that emphasis should be placed on the intellectual virtues as the purpose of higher education, if it is understood that intellectual virtue is a means for the cultivation of moral virtue, and character is a by-product of the training of both intellect and will. Moral virtue and character training must accompany intellectual development if the end product is to be "a man thoroughly reasonable; a man whose character is unified; a man in whom intellectual and moral virtues working harmoniously together can produce, insofar as it can be produced, that perfect contemplation of supreme truth which is the beginning of beatitude here and its consummation hereafter." [1]

Here again we run into the problem of keeping two ideas in one's mind at the same time, and maintaining a proper balance between the two, realizing that one is a complement of the other and that neither can be separated from the other without damaging the whole concept.

The following is an excerpt from a newspaper report on a discussion of the same problem:

Intellectual aims of education "unjustifiably" place obstacles in the way of "an unfolding student apostolate," it was charged at the Study Week in Davenport.

The charge was made by Rev. Robert S. Pelton, C.S.C., who also said it seems that restriction of intellectual aims of education to exclude student apostolate activities "in certain cases at least" is done "to save the educators trouble."

The "intellectual line" is that "we are here to teach principles; application comes later," Father Pelton said, adding:

[1] Very Reverend Gerald E. Dupont, S.S.E., The Proper Aims of the Catholic College in Affiliation Bulletin for Institutions of Higher Education, XV 3 (February, 1953), p. 5.

"Talk of this kind used to make John Dewey shudder, but since that would not impress most Catholic educators, it is worth reminding them that Dewey stands firmly with Aristotle and Saint Thomas here. If a principle has any kind of bearing on life, Aristotle and Aquinas contend that we could never be said to have learned it until we could apply it."

The Holy Cross priest said it is charged against the student apostolate that its "principles are too idealistic."

The Christian humanist must be prepared "to challenge the cynical realist on his own ground—of realism." He must show that he recognizes "the complexity of his principles as they bear on a human situation; that he is fully aware of the role of persuasion, of his own need to learn from experience and obstacles—learn more deeply the meaning of his concrete principles."

But, Father Pelton said, such an attitude cannot evolve from the classroom alone or from "bull sessions." It needs the experience of "setting up a book exchange, organizing visiting workshops to under-privileged areas and homes, planning imaginative social events, teaching CCD classes."

He gave the example of YCS group which was studying race problems and which volun-

teered to solicit signatures for a non-discrimina-
tory real estate policy.

"The face-to-face reaction of homeowners
gave them an insight into social bias that would
have been impossible to garner from reading or
discussion among themselves."

Too many priests, brothers, and sisters,
Father Pelton said, "are forsaking the hard work
of a formative experience for the more grati-
fying way of personal friendship."

A great deal, of course, has been written on
the nature and meaning of Catholic higher education but it will mean little if Catholic educators do
not try to effect what is being preached. The basic
necessity for accomplishing this is the establishment
of a faculty the individual members of which themselves are living examples of the product of a true
Catholic education. This, of course, is not an easy
task, but administrators of institutions of Catholic
higher education must keep everlastingly at the task.
Evidence exists of a defeatist's attitude toward the
problem. "It is impossible to get teachers of this
kind; we must get the best available and be satisfied
with them," is the way the thinking goes. We may
have to make use of material which is less than what
we desire, but we must never be satisfied with it.
We must not let our ideals in such an important task
become dulled. Catholic educators must work constantly at this problem. In fact, the difficulty will

not cease to exist until we have an appreciable number of Catholic institutions which have solved it to a large extent, from whose graduates administrators of other Catholic colleges and universities can draw prospective members of their own teaching staffs.

The following is the statement of the purpose of a Catholic college for men, which may be regarded as typical for or at least befitting all Catholic colleges for men.

"College exists for the students and offers to them the opportunity for self-realization. Education is the process by which this is accomplished. Liberal education is the process by which it is best accomplished, because liberal education looks to the development of the whole man and of all his faculties.

"Education is primarily directed to the development of the mind. To open the student's mind to the whole realm of truth, to enlighten and strengthen his reason, to develop as fully as possible his powers to think, is specifically the work of the College. Nothing is allowed to distract from this essential aim.

"Education as a process of growth is not complete, however, and is ineffective, unless mental development is accompanied by the development of virtue and good character. A Catholic institution would indeed find it difficult to justify its existence if it did not strive to permeate all its activity with the spirit of Christ and with the ideals of conduct and religious life which are found in His teaching. In striving for the development of virtue and good character in the students, furthermore, the College is carrying on the highest traditions of liberal education. True liberal education has always sought the formation not only of the intelligent man, but of the good man.

"The College also believes that liberal education has never been and should not be divorced from the practical needs of life. The 'ivory tower' concept of education for leisure is not realistic in twentieth century America. Since most of our students do not belong to the leisure class, they are understandably interested in securing some kind of gainful occupation soon after their graduation, unless they go on to professional studies. This is a reasonable objective, but the whole concept of liberal education and indeed the purpose of life itself can be vitiated and made meaningless, if material gain is made the primary aim.

"Students, in their impatience and eagerness to become vocationally competent, are inclined to take the view that the shortest path is the best. They become restless under the disciplines which are called 'humanistic,' unless they can be made to understand that, in the long range view, such studies are of great importance even for vocational plans. They must be made to see that where technical competence is without direction and without firm anchorage in fundamental principles, accumulation of wealth is paralleled by the decay of men.

"Sound vocational education should be based upon broad foundations of knowledge. Ways of speaking and writing, the ability to get at once to the heart of a problem found in a book, a report, or an analysis, knowledge of human motivation, knowledge of oneself and others, are necessary for promotions and advancements in business. But no one can develop these abilities or acquire this knowledge in a few weeks or a few months. Psychology, theology, economics, literature, history are the sources which have to be tapped.

Experience teaches that the development of the student's intellectual capacities by the discipline of the liberal arts and sciences is the very best way of preparing him for the practical life. Specialized training for specific occupations may be required, but it will be made easier, quicker, more lasting, and more productive when founded upon liberal education. To become a resourceful person, alert and responsive to varying demands, trained for all sorts of jobs in general and for one field in particular, requires a preparation and a point of view which come only from a deep and careful self cultivation. These facts are becoming more and more clearly recognized by medical and dental schools, by law schools, by schools of engineering, by business corporations, and even by the directors of military training schools. It might well be added here that sound vocational training with a background of liberal arts enables a person to serve others effectively, thus fulfilling his general vocation as a Christian."

The essence of all Catholic education is contained in the description presented above. *Mutatis mutandis* it applies to all levels of Catholic education. In general, the sharp difference between the meaning of Catholic and non-Catholic education is to be found in two respects, i.e. the emphasis on the training of the whole man and the special attention given to the development of the good man, in its Christian and Catholic meaning.

The success of Catholic educators in attaining these ends within the field of higher education has been noteworthy but all in all hardly satisfactory enough. By discussing some of the outstanding problems involved it is hoped that this book will be of noteworthy value in spreading the true meaning of Catholic higher education and in helping to implement it.

CHAPTER THREE

THE RESPONSIBILITIES OF THE GENERAL COLLEGE AND PROFESSIONAL EDUCATION

Before discussing the responsibilities of the general college to professional education, it is necessary to explain the term "General College." This is indeed an unpleasant task, since no greater unanimity of opinion has been reached regarding it than exists on the definition of the term "College of Liberal Arts." The irony of this state of affairs can be appreciated, when you recall that the name "General College" was first devised in order to avoid the difficulty of having to define the "College of Liberal Arts." Indeed, many educators today would identify the two types of institutions.

Perhaps we will fare best if we attempt first to define the College of Liberal Arts, and in doing so we will be obliged to use terms which are quite familiar to all. The College of Liberal Arts aims to train men who are truly free, that is, men who in relation to the outside world will be able to adjust themselves properly and easily to the surroundings in which they may find themselves, whatever these may be; who will be able to meet misfortune as well as success in a manner that will give them complete satisfaction. In other words, the truly liberally educated person will be able to rise above the vicissitudes of daily life and keep at peace with himself. This external calm, however, is only indicative of an inner peace or contentment which arises from his relationship with his God and Creator. Through his liberal studies, he has come to know Him as never before. He has penetrated the order of the universe and he knows his place in it. Moreover, he sees nothing strange about all this. What his God expects of him he regards as quite natural and perfectly just, as justice itself, and he is most eager to carry out his part to the fullest in the order of the universe.

The College of Liberal Arts develops such a man by training him to think, and by giving him the principles by which he thinks properly, and by giving him an abundance of material on which to exercise and perfect himself in the use of these principles. The fact that the College of Liberal Arts has on the whole, as some educators think, failed seriously in the last several generations to achieve its purposes does not change our definition.

The principles, and to a less extent the material with which to exercise these principles, must come from the three fields of theology, philosophy, and history, and in that order of importance, the three and the only fields of knowledge that cut across all other fields. Obviously, the success with which a college of liberal arts attains its objectives will depend to the greatest extent on how well these three fields of knowledge are taught and integrated with the rest of the curriculum. The college will pay a terrific price in the quality of its product, if it waters down or cuts corners in its instruction here. The remaining fields of learning will contribute to or perhaps rather help to confirm the principles involved, but their role is chiefly to broaden the student's experience by furnishing material, peculiar to themselves, on which to work. Good results, of course, cannot be obtained by closely restricting the number or variety of these fields, but, on the other hand, there is real danger in too much and too superficial diversification. A well-planned program of studies which will give genuinely deep knowledge of one field with more limited experience in a number of related fields, all over and above the basic triad of theology, philosophy, and history, and determined by giving due consideration to the aptitude and personal interests of the student, best achieves the ends of a liberal education.

The so-called General College looks to these very same ends. It differs from the College of Liberal Arts in the importance which it places on the various fields of knowledge for achieving these desired objectives. At this point it becomes necessary to call attention to a very important fact which educators have come to realize at all fully only in recent years. Outside of the three fields of theology, philosophy, and history, which taken together have a very special part to play in the college curriculum, no field or group of fields has a monopoly on the ability to train for a liberal education. Here we find the greatest divergence between the two types of institutions now under consideration.

The supporters of the College of Liberal Arts will insist on languages and literatures, some, even today, on the traditional Greek and Latin languages and literatures, as indispensable for a program of studies in the college of liberal arts. Many, furthermore, would eschew any subject which is in any way chiefly concerned with developing a skill in a profession, to say nothing of any of the subjects now referred to by educators as the practical arts and sciences. Even the natural sciences have only in comparatively recent years come into their own as instruments for the training of liberally educated people. This is reflected in the reluctance with which many colleges give the degree of bachelor of arts, still the only symbol of a liberal education, to those who have placed the chief emphasis in their program of studies on a natural science, or to those who have failed to include a pitiful year or two of Latin in their college program. They have, of course, long since given up on the Greek, although the general bantering about the uselessness of Greek as a college subject still goes on. While the traces of these hidebound ideas can still be seen in the thinking of educators in so-called colleges of liberal arts, the tendency to greater liberality in recognizing various fields of specialization within their institutions as important for the attaining of a liberal education is growing ever stronger.

At this point, I think it well to quote the Revised Manual of Accreditation, North Central Association of Colleges and Secondary Schools: "For purposes of accreditation the term 'general education' signifies acquaintance with the major areas of knowledge; it implies possession of the facts in such areas and some proficiency in the modes of thought involved in understanding such facts. In its purpose and its content it is a continuation of the kind of education offered in secondary schools. It excludes definite vocational preparation."

Those who profess the type of educational institution known as the General College have long since definitely broken with the idea of the indispensability of the classical languages and literatures for a program of studies which aims to produce the "free man." They have for a long period enthusiastically accepted the natural sciences as an effective means to this end. With varying degrees of willingness they are ready to introduce the professions and many of the vocations into the curriculums of their institutions. Yet with all these strong differences from the College of Liberal Arts, the General College, it must be remembered, is quite serious in its claims to success in producing the "free man."

Thus far I have said nothing new on the subject and frankly some may be slightly cynical about the validity of this aim for our institution of higher education. Surely, there is some good ground for cynicism as far as the actual achievement of this purpose is concerned. Just examine any group of college catalogues collected at random and read the optimistic accounts of the aims and purposes of these institutions. Actually, we know from distressing experiences that non-sectarian colleges, in an honest effort to be really non-sectarian, have in every way possible deleted or attenuated teaching on religious and philosophical subjects, and they have of necessity thereby failed woefully in giving the student the most fundamental knowledge upon which he may develop his thinking so as to become truly free. Except for sporadic, but futile, attempts to strengthen instruction for this purpose, colleges have for the most part tried to avoid the issue by resorting to the teaching of apparent facts, and, if philosophical principles are introduced, they are of the kind characteristic of the relativistic school of thought. "The principles seem to be true today; they may possibly be false tomorrow," is the way the thinking goes, a very uncertain foundation indeed upon which a man is to develop his guiding plan so as to be "free." Sectarian institutions of higher education, especially those of the Catholic faith, have a great advantage here, but it is highly doubtful that they have made full use of it.

We have said enough probably to refresh your minds on the nature of the General College. To repeat, its aim is to produce the free man, free to make sound decisions in his relations with the outside world, so that he may be free within himself to enjoy the peace of the grace of God.

As I have said, the advocates of the General College believe that a very wide variety of fields of learning can contribute to the process of producing the free man. They definitely include the studies of the professional fields among these. Perhaps the most prominent Catholic educator of this group was the late Father Edward Leen, an English Redemptorist Father. He once said: "History, it is true, shows that many men and women, too, have achieved that distinction of mind and will and manner which goes to constitute *personality* in the

accepted sense of the term. But such men and women are exceptions. For the vast majority of mankind, stunted lives and underfed souls are the
consequences of material want. As surely as plants
and shrubs become shriveled and stunted when ex-
posed to constant east winds, so surely do the con-
tinual fear and uncertainty that agitate those whose
daily bread is not secure, impede growth of the
soul." [1]

And a little later he adds: "The imparting of
these abilities that make for professional success,
when the studies and activities proper to a profession
are undertaken, and the forming of an intelligent
economic sense, are an important element in education. They are, however, far from being the most
important. A livelihood but lays the foundation of a
human life. The superstructure is the paramount
thing. The parts and the form, and the embellish-
ment of this superstructure are the main concern of
the educative process. When a man has secured
economic independence, there lies before him the
great work to which he is called by the Author of his
living and by the inner promptings of his own soul.
God bids him achieve an excellent human life. He
himself aspires after a life that shall be eminently
satisfying and satisfactory. God bids him make for
happiness, even in this world. He himself ardently

[1] Reverend Edward Leen, What is Education? (New York:
Sheed and Ward, 1943) p. 12.

desires to secure happiness even through such experience as lies on this side of the grave. Strangely
enough, he can succeed in gaining the relative but
real happiness that is attainable in spite of the apparent obstacles presented by the order of things
around him. His success depends on his bringing
his vision as to the meaning of human life, and as
to the meaning of the material universe placed at
the disposal of man for the purpose of human living,
into harmony with the views of God with regard to
the very same things. The principal work of the educator, as such, is to utilize all the means at his disposal, offered by art, science, literature, and revelation to effect the harmony." [2]

We quite agree with Father Leen, but we would
add a few warnings which we feel certain Father
Leen himself would have supported. Every college
which would achieve its purposes effectively must
constantly bear in mind what each course contributes to the final product to be achieved by the
entire curriculum. In addition to specific content
of any course, what that course contributes to the
producing of the free man must be borne in mind.
No course can justify itself unless it makes a satisfactory record on both of these counts. In general,
this involves giving a course from the historical and
humanistic points of view, and naturally requires
an instructor who has himself been liberally

[2] Ibid., p. 2, 3.

educated and who thus can appreciate and carry out these important features of the course. There ought to be no great difficulty in procuring such teachers for the non-professional or general courses, but unfortunately with education having been slanted for several years toward early narrow specialization and with little attention having been paid to the program as a whole, the teaching profession on the higher level is becoming filled with anything but the liberally trained teachers. It is to be hoped that with some of the foremost colleges of the land taking the lead in reforming their curriculums, looking to the development of truly liberally educated graduates, this condition may soon be at least improved. But it is a much more difficult task to find liberally educated teachers for professional subjects. We do not, however, consider this an impossible task, and, if the General College will see its duty toward the professions and perform it adequately, this problem also will be resolved. Much progress has already been made along this line in the field of business education and in the various branches of the engineering profession.

But to return to the General College strictly, the duty of this institution in American society, even more than of any other academic entity, is to turn out liberally educated citizens. This is its traditional responsibility and it grows greater with the years. It grows greater in expanse by reason of the fact that the general level of education throughout the land is being pushed up from graduation from a secondary school to the satisfactory completion of at least two years of college work. The conviction also is growing everywhere that it is a very valuable asset in life to be equipped with the training of a full four-year college program, and more and more of our American youth are striving to achieve this very thing. The responsibility of the general college is increasing also by reason of the more manifold results which it is expected to accomplish in its graduates. We might call this an increase in qualitative responsibility. Thus, it is expected to turn out citizens who will not fall an easy prey to false philosophies, such as communism, as they have done in the recent past. They must contribute in large measure to the breaking down of prejudices of all kinds, especially those of race and creed. The democracy of fifth century Athens was probably the most successful experiment in democratic government up to our time, but it failed because it refused full citizenship and equal rights to everyone who was not a full-blooded Athenian. Who can honestly say that the prejudices abroad in our land today, which, while pretending to offer equal rights to citizens of certain racial minorities through cleverly devised subterfuges are actually scheming to deny them, are not a serious menace to our own democracy? The teachings of our institutions of higher education are our greatest hope for the dispelling of these insidious influences. Whether the American General College can meet this challenge on the qualitative side and especially the responsibility of training more effectively for good citizenship remains to be seen.

The magnitude of the responsibility of the American General College is increased still more by the general conviction of most educators that the professions cannot train successfully outside the confines of the professions themselves. Training for the free man, that is, the good citizen in the best sense of the term, must be done by the General College. Indeed, some educators in the professions are willing to agree that the professions will achieve better practitioners by reason of their having been trained simultaneously to be good representatives of American citizenship and truly free men. While being trained to be expert followers of a profession, they must also learn the responsibilities which go with that knowledge. Thus the General College, to perform its true service to society, must face conditions as they are today and adopt a broad outlook as to the nature of its curriculums. It definitely cannot stick stubbornly, as a few still attempt to do, to the narrow and strictly traditional point of view. As a matter of fact, in spite of what a great many catalogues say, most colleges are attempting to adjust themselves to the broader outlook on the ways and means of attaining the traditional product of a free man. In other words, they are trying to find a place in their various programs of study for training in or for the professions. However, much still remains to be done on both sides of this problem before anything like a successful solution can be said to have been reached.

There may be a question as to what is meant by "on both sides of the problem." On the one side of the problem is the general educator, and on the other side is the educator in professional fields. Only when they both see eye to eye on the nature of the so-called professional programs in the general college, can we give a truly successful training in the professions to our students.

First of all, both must realize that to attain the end described no courses should be regarded as strictly general or strictly professional. All courses must contribute as much as possible to the total effect of the entire program, and this must always be kept in mind by both types of educators. The general educator in planning his so-called non-professional courses, should work with the educator in professional subjects to contribute through these courses every possible benefit to the professional aspects of the students' training without divesting the course of any of its cultural or purely intellectual values. For example, it is difficult to see what is to be gained by insisting on a general course in chemistry, for nurses, which was intended originally as the first step in a long series of courses directed toward the training of a research chemist or a chemical engineer. Likewise, it is difficult to see what is to be lost, if the course in chemistry, without abandoning its challenge to the students' intellect, is organized so as to appeal to the nurse by its appropriate advertense to the nursing profession. Personally I am not sympathetic with special history courses, such as the history of chemistry, the history of social work, and the history of nursing, except as they are deemed necessary to fill an unavoidable gap. The story of the development of nursing, for example, as a profession would mean much more if given as a part of a regular course in history, tied together with all the other phases of the history of civilization. At one time history was taught as a record of political events, as little more than chronology. Today it is taught as a study of the entire civilization of a people, including its social and economic phases. A course in general history intended primarily for nurses or members of other professions should bring in the developments in the profession in question, showing how it was necessarily affected by contemporary events and existing leadership. I see great possibilities here, if carried out according to the true historical method and with close and sympathetic cooperation and good judgment on the part of the general educator and the nurse educator. At present, the surface of the problem has been barely scratched.

The general educator also should be alert to recognize latent cultural values in the so-called professional courses, and the educator in the professions should not be averse to modifying these courses so as to increase their cultural and purely intellectual benefits without in turn damaging the required professional knowledge or skill which must be imparted. Whenever we speak in this vein we are at once faced with the so-called courses in the nursing arts, the one kind of course which is supposedly completely impervious to any cultural or liberal influence. But even nursing arts can be taught with proper emphasis on the reason for doing these important tasks in one way rather than in another, and can be taken as probably the best opportunity for driving home the fundamental ethical principle that it is the patient's welfare and every comfort that always receives the good nurse's first consideration. All this can certainly qualify the course in nursing arts to receive college credit in a program of studies aimed at producing the "free" man just as much as the recently developed courses in physical education which have in many institutions taken on a new seriousness. Similarly, the other professional courses, if given by well trained teachers can be adjusted with little difficulty so as to contribute still more to the final product of the integrated program. But again, the director of the profession has got to believe in *all* the objectives of his program of studies, and has to be concerned about the contribution which the purely professional courses can make to the general aims as well as to the particular professional objectives.

Continuing to think in terms of a truly unified program, there are other considerations than those of the curriculum which the administrators of the General College must take seriously in relation to the professors. I shall mention a few that come to mind, and, although I shall present them with illustrations from nursing, my arguments will be equally applicable to any of the other professions.

The impact of a group of nurses on the social life of a college, especially a small college which perhaps has been operating somewhat in the spirit of a select finishing school, regularly creates a problem. Judging from reports that have come to me, there is a tendency to treat the professional group as a separate entity within the social frame-work of the institution. This seems to me to be a mistake and a serious handicap to the achievement of the ultimate aims of the college. Obviously, the entire student body of a college must be treated as a *single* entity, socially as well as academically. Small groups may well have special functions of their own but never to the extent that these functions in the slightest degree rival those of the college as a whole. The social functions of a college have an important part to play in the welding of the entire student body into a single unit, and they also have a mature and broadening effect upon the students, which comes from persons of varying interests rubbing elbows with one another. The administrators of the General College must beware lest any group within the college begin to regard itself as the most important part of the institution, if not really the institution itself, and at the same time they should not entirely repress or ignore these groups. Frankly, there does not seem to be any serious problem here which a little ingenuity and tact cannot handle.

Closely allied to the problem of social integration is that of participation in extra-curricular activities. Again, it is a mistake to assume that the nurses or any other professional group are too busy to take part in such affairs, and then proceed to ignore them completely as far as their being possible participants in these activities is concerned. The approach here is similar to that above. Every effort should be made to enable all students, regardless of their academic interests, to procure the benefits that come from these extracurricular activities. Ordinarily, all these extracurricular affairs should be those of the college as a whole, and there should be few, if any, open only to a particular section of the student body. To cite an actual example the college glee club should be truly representative of the entire college; it should not be necessary to conduct a special glee club for the nursing students. Here again there does not appear to be any serious difficulties which a good administrator cannot handle.

College administrators together with the directors of professional subjects should cooperate in detecting students of special ability and promise, who should either go on to further study in the professional field beyond what the College has to offer or even to transfer to an entirely different field. Similarly, students who for some reason are quite unfit for the profession in which they are being trained should, likewise, be noted early and properly advised. All this, to be sure, is a guidance problem, but I wish to point out that much more satisfactory results could be obtained from the judgments of people with different points of view than would result from the judgment of the director of the professional studies alone. Furthermore, the General College which is not committed to any specific and narrow training for its students has the responsibility of contributing its broader and more varied experience in the field of guidance to the professional groups within the college family as well as to the others.

In the final analysis, it seems to me that it is the responsibility of the general college, if it decides to set up an integrated professional program among its offerings, to adopt such a curriculum with genuine confidence that it will attain the same general

aims as all the other curriculums of the institution
and at the same time provide for the special objectives of the professions. If the administrators of the
general college feel that the demands of the profession concerned are so incompatible with their
general aims that this cannot be done, they should
not attempt to offer such a program. I believe this
to be particularly true for Catholic colleges. It is
difficult for me to understand how Catholic educators can justify offering any academic program
whose first objective is not that of the general college as I have already described it. I believe, however, that with a clear understanding of the problem
on the part of all concerned satisfactory curriculums
can be worked out with essentially any of the professions. Actually, a program of studies of this kind,
developed as I have attempted to explain, should
send forth better members of the professions in
every way, better in the strictly professional sense,
and better in the sense of men and women of refine-
ment and Catholic leaders.

CHAPTER FOUR

THE CHALLENGE OF THE CATHOLIC COLLEGE FOR WOMEN TODAY

The Catholic college for women as a group has made tremendous progress, both in numbers and quality of instruction and training. It got its start nearly a hundred years later than the Catholic college for men but in total number and in the number approved by the recognized accrediting groups, i.e. the regional associations and the professional groups, they far outstrip the Catholic colleges for men. However, probably from the very rapidity of their growth they have taken on in some instances certain serious weaknesses. Many religious communities for women live for the day when they can open a college of their own, and sometimes hasten the day long before they have the resources of personnel and actual funds to do so properly. There is at least one case on record of a religious community of moderate size, which was conducting several successful secondary schools but no institution of higher education, closing all but one and establishing a college, and then in the face of threatening disaster suddenly awakening to the fact, which they should have known in the first place, that vocations to the religious life among women usually develop in girlhood while attending secondary schools. With this supply of vocations cut off and only slightly compensated by college students, this religious community was in dire straits!

When a group attempts to establish a college with meagre resources, the following weaknesses, among others, usually arise: a faculty whose members are poorly trained and who, because of their small number, are obliged to carry excessive teaching loads, far beyond the demands of good policy; programs of study whose offerings cannot always be given because of lack of teaching personnel or whose electives, which are important for meeting the individual desires and talents of students, are essentially non-existent; poor libraries as collections of books, lacking suitable materials for supplementary study in courses; and an inadequate social and cultural life.

The fact that so many Catholic colleges for women have grown out of academies or in very close contact with them, and that the administrative experience of those who conduct them has been confined chiefly to secondary schools, has also been a source of certain serious short-comings in these colleges. Reference is had here to both the intellectual standards and to the proper concepts of an appropriate social life. In this connection I am happy to recall a large and well known religious community which attempted to establish a college by training the veteran teaching staff of the academy personnel and making use of the old building in which the secondary school was housed. To the credit of the superiors, the futility of this plan soon became evident, and, in spite of the expense involved, a plot of land was purchased several miles distant from the academy, and a series of modern college buildings was erected, young sisters with little experience in teaching in the secondary school and still pliable in their thought processes were trained for college teaching, and a college was set up with little or no influence from the old academy tradition. On the other hand too many of our Catholic colleges for women have been unable for one or a combination of the reasons given above to break away from the baleful deterrents of past experience.

At this point I would like to ask the administrators of Catholic colleges for women why it is that so few religious vocations arise among graduates of our Catholic colleges of women. I have asked a large number of sisters this question during my experience and the following is the gist of the answers. "The girls lose respect for the educators and administrative officers who have to do so many chores not compatible with their collegiate status, such as acting as floor supervisors in dormitories, switchboard operators, and others. They naturally raise the question why these duties are not given to others, lay or religious, who are not trained to fill college positions, and the college personnel given that time to study and keep up with the latest thinking in their fields. The modern young women are "fed up" with the finishing school approach to teaching and the naïveté of some of the Sisters who are assigned to college work. They have a tendency to admire lay personnel and criticize the Sisters many of whom act very unprofessionally."

Another serious defect in many of our Catholic colleges for women is the lack of a good guidance program. The traditional practice of placing anyone, especially a laywoman who has raised a family of her own, in charge of such a responsibility is no longer acceptable. The program of guidance in college is a professional activity, and as such requires some one professionally trained to direct it. This day of an increasing number of broken homes with the consequent psychological problems inflicted on the children makes it necessary that competently trained persons be placed in charge of the work.

I do not wish to give the impression that we do not have a good proportion of Catholic colleges for women which can meet the exacting demands of specialists in modern higher education. They are among us and can be named. I wish only to call attention to the fact that we still have too many which are still living in the past and as yet have not taken the first step toward the development of an outstanding modern college for women.

The main purpose, however, in my presenting this chapter is to call the attention of our Catholic women educators to the need of a thorough study of the purposes of a Catholic college for women today and an objective review of their purposes. What does the Catholic woman of today most need by way of a college training in order to perform her part best in the expanding areas for women in American life? The following statement from Cardinal Suenens [1] is very much to the point:

"Freed from her former shackles, she evolves in an atmosphere that allows her to deploy her natural gifts. Greater life-expectation gives her, once her children are grown up, an extra life, as it were. The culture available to her is wider and she

---

[1] *The Nun in the World*, Westminster, Maryland, 1963, p. 13.

has more leisure. All these new factors affect her position and her activities in the world and open them to almost unlimited extension."

Let us hope that our Catholic women educators will rise to this challenge. Certainly in my own lifetime, several far-sighted nuns, although laboring largely in isolation, are meeting this challenge nobly.

Some believe that the Catholic woman can find the college training best suited for her in a Catholic co-educational institution, and this has caused some consternation among the administrators of Catholic colleges for women, conjuring up as it does, the possible extinction of the Catholic college for women. On the contrary, it seems to me, the challenge presented here, if properly met, will establish the Catholic college for women in its appropriate and secure place. The modern Catholic college for women, as I envision it, while necessarily presenting many courses over-lapping in content those of the co-educational institutions, should be permeated throughout by a philosophy directed strongly to the presentation of woman's place and responsibility in modern society. This, of course, would be difficult to achieve in a co-educational institution.

CHAPTER FIVE

THE PROBLEM OF RESEARCH IN CATHOLIC INSTITUTIONS OF HIGHER EDUCATION

An item on the program, "What would you say?," presented at the meeting of the Middle States Association of Colleges and Secondary Schools, held during Thanksgiving Week, 1960, is the following:

Faculty: The team which visited a college says: "Although faculty morale and classroom performance are good, there are danger signs ahead. Only twenty--one percent of the faculty have doctorates compared with thirty percent ten years ago. There is little evidence of active faculty scholarship."

The college replies: While of course we want a scholarly faculty, our objectives emphasize teaching not research. We are not convinced that faculty research leads to better teaching."

I am convinced for reasons of my own that the the reference here is to a Catholic college, although the fallacious judgment involved will be met in non-Catholic colleges as well.

We have here another of those academic questions which persist in cropping up periodically. While this particular question seems again and again to have been answered satisfactorily, the answers are soon forgotten or seem never to have been accepted in the first place. This is probably due to the fact that a genuine interest in research and a willingness to submit to the rigid discipline of training for or in research is common to comparatively few people, many of whom have a genuine desire to teach but are unwilling to train for their profession properly. Yet we must not overlook the problem of the shortage of teachers, both religious and lay, which brings about heavy teaching loads and so deprives them of the necessary time for research. At any rate, as a result of this wide-spread attitude a feeling has developed that teaching and research are incompatible, and qualities of good teaching and characteristics of genuine research search have become greatly confused. The teachers and administrators of some colleges, usually inferior ones, talk glibly about their students being thoroughly trained in and doing research when they have reference to the most elementary investigation of secondary sources.

We believe that teaching and research are essentially necessary to each other, if good training and worthwhile research are properly understood. The idea of research has unfortunately become associated in men's minds with a highly artificial process of investigation, with deep and narrow specialization, and too infrequently, I fear, with an activity, while regarded as beneficial to mankind in a vague kind of way, is actually carried on only by a very small number of queer people in ivory towers. Research, by being associated with the university, as one of its two chief functions, has become involved in a great deal of philosophizing on the nature of a university and in particular on the idea of a Catholic university. I have no intention whatsoever of belittling these serious philosophical studies of the nature of research. I mention them merely to show how different is my own view in this matter. I believe that mankind suffers a great loss when it fails to note that the idea of research is essentially very simple, and properly understood should pervade all man's intellectual activities to his everlasting benefit.

Research is the systematic search for truth. We should never permit ourselves to get away from this very clear and simple notion. Of course, it must be said that the procedures for the search for truth may differ greatly from one another in different fields, and may become very complex, but the one all important end of these procedures is the same. When scholars in the past tried to distinguish between pure research and applied research on the basis of searching for truth for its own sake and searching for some truth through which by some particular discovery wealth might be acquired, they were only complicating matters needlessly. That men intended to acquire money by their search for truth, either to keep together their bodies and souls or to enjoy the very possession of wealth for its own sake, may very well be an ethical question, but it does not affect our simple definition, "Research is the systematic search for truth." Nor is our definition affected by the nature of the truth for which we search, whether it be a new method of searching for truth in some narrow field, or a new plan for laying mines to defend our shores against the enemy, or a hitherto unknown process, cheap and easy, for producing petroleum, or anything else. Research is still the systematic search for truth, and it may be said to take place in countless operations in everyday life and especially in nearly every well-conducted activity of the classroom.

Similarly, our definition should not be complicated by abstruse considerations of the relationship of research to the spirit and spiritual things. Here also we can continue to speak in simple terms. If we do not believe in God or the workings of His grace, but like the Pelagians believe that we accomplish all by the power of our own minds with no help from any one else, not even Him Who is the Author of all, we evolve into strange mortals indeed, warped minds incapable of making a proper use of the new knowledge which we acquire. Our research, however, is still the systematic search for truth. On the other hand, with proper humility, conscious always of our debt to the Author of all, the research experiences of our daily lives can enrich and promote our spiritual evolution. This is all very clear and easy to understand as the many who have shared in this experience will testify. This spiritual phase of the search for truth does not vitiate in the slightest the scientific nature of the research involved but rather makes the particular research exercise complete. Moreover, it confirms the claim for research as the basis of all real education.

This simple thought of searching for truth and doing so by a logical process should be the underlying principle of education from the kindergarten to the very end of the educational system. It is difficult to see how we can have successful education without it. If the teacher gives due attention always to the workings of divine grace in men's lives, even in his search for truth, this principle becomes a most effective instrument for imparting a religious education. God is truth. Man must always be seeking truth if he would obtain the place for which he longs. Therefore, it behooves him to acquire the method and the habit of seeking truth successfully. Inadequate as this statement is, it is sufficient perhaps to illustrate the possibilities for successful teaching through this simple principle at any stage in the process of education. Now you may say that this has essentially always been done in our schools, and I would agree with you to a certain extent, but a serious weakness in our present educational procedure is the failure to recognize and to proclaim it openly. In none of the early stages of his education, at least, is the student made properly conscious of its nature and of the importance of his understanding it so well that it becomes a part of his own nature. The teacher must strive for this constantly from the beginning to the end.

Unfortunately, the principle of research is not recognized as such until the student has reached at least the secondary school. By failing to recognize it up to that point and by being unaware of the contribution which it can make in both the spiritual and the intellectual development of the student, the teacher misses the opportunity to be especially helpful to the student during the most sensitive and educative period of his life. Worse still, the teacher too often not only completely ignores this principle but reduces his teaching to merely insisting that the pupil accept all statements without question and to making him memorize them for parrot-like recitation when called upon. The teacher not infrequently performs his function by rote, not by stimulating thinking and following the research principle. The teacher may even pull the term "research" out of a hat, as it were, presenting it as a most interesting and attractive experience, and then introduce the students to that most demoralizing process of reading what others have said on a certain subject, copying another's words with little or no change, even including the punctuation, sometimes splicing the sentences of one author with those of another, and then presenting this naive pilfering as a highly laudable and academic exercise. This atrocious procedure the student is taught to call the process of research.

Now I am not so foolish as to think that we can make experts in research out of students in the years of childhood and adolescence, but I do insist that we can train them to think at least with some degree of accuracy from the earliest school years. We must not, as is often done, sell the intellectual ability of the students short. We can also teach them with ever increasing effectiveness what good scholarship and research is and develop in them a genuine respect for it. We must instill in them a keen sense of intellectual honesty, an abhorrence for anything that smacks of deception. All this I submit is of the nature of good research in its proper and very simple significance, and unless we are successful in inculcating it, we fall short that much in achieving the only acceptable end of good teaching, the ability and eagerness to search for truth. Furthermore, if our thinking can in any way be regarded as sound, it makes the rather common assertion and even boast of some teachers, that their interest is in teaching and not at all in research a gross absurdity.

There are some practical assets to be gained by the teacher in research, several of which should be mentioned here. The teacher will have acquired an almost instinctive ability to gauge a work of professed scholarship, both its weaknesses and its strengths. He will be a more reliable judge as to what new material should be introduced into the substance of his course. The teacher trained in research will be able to distinguish carefully between fact and theory and so to present his material more accurately. He will not set forth all things as facts, as so many do, but, as the occasion demands, will be able to describe several theories as possible facts but as yet not convincingly established. He will be able to impart to his students that most important attitude towards knowledge: so little of our general information is absolute fact and so much of it deserves serious consideration as possible fact. Finally, he will be able to organize the material of his course in a manner that will bring out comparative values.

Even in presenting a bibliography, works of second-ary importance containing little or no original think-ing will not appear on the same plane with pioneer and original investigations of outstanding impor-tance, at least not without pertinent comment.

There are, to be sure, certain scholars, although I believe that they are few in number, who have little sympathy with teaching. Most of the genuine scholars with whom I have been acquainted have always welcomed the opportunity to teach at least a little. In fact, the most inspiring and personally beneficial teachers whom I have ever had, have been outstanding scholars. The very process of teaching may be very helpful to the scholar in his research activity. In arranging for class presentation, ideas are often clarified and relationships suddenly appear which were lost in the intensive thinking of the research laboratory or the library. Even students of little experience in scholarly investigation may individually present stimulating and even important ideas, and their reactions as a group to scientific speculation may be very helpful to the scholar. Per-haps, most important of all is the genuine satifaction which the true scholar receives from sharing his new knowledge with others in a personal way, all of which is impossible in the concentrated attention which he must give to his investigations when alone by himself.

But what should be the attitude toward research on the part of the average teacher, who all too often does not have enough time even to organize his courses or to review new material?

(1) First of all, I would hope that all teachers on whatever level will have had experience with enough good teachers to appreciate what the over-all research process is and to value it properly.

(2) If what I have just said is to any great extent true, it would be reasonable to expect that they would be able to adapt the over-all process of research to their teaching successfully on whatever level it may be.

(3) Here I would interpose a negative statement. I would never expect to hear a derogatory statement about research or one boasting of a lack of interest in it from any truly successful teacher.

(4) I would expect all sincere effective teachers to belong to at least one scholarly association and to receive at least one scientific journal in order to keep himself abreast of the latest accomplishments in his field.

(5) Also, for keeping himself informed, I would expect to see a good teacher attend at least one annual meeting, either local or national, of the teachers or scholars of his special field.

(6) I would not necessarily expect much deeply scholarly material from every successful teacher, although such productivity is by no means unknown

on the part of busy teachers, but I would look for occasional brief comments or an article even if it involved only pertinent observations and first-hand experience in his field.

For a teacher to permit himself to fall into a rut, handing out the same information in the same way year after year, is the death knell of good teaching. The statement in the quotation made at the beginning of this paper, namely, "We are not convinced that faculty research leads to better teaching," coming as it does from a college administrator, is nothing less than pitiful and bodes ill for the future of that college. Unfortunately, I have good reason to believe that it comes from a Catholic college.

Unfortunately also, in spite of much discussion and the presentation of striking evidence in support of teaching with some backing of research principles, it is very questionable that any great progress is being made with this problem. I wish to close this chapter with the following excerpt from a recent Middle States evaluation report which I am taking the liberty of quoting from "The Middle States Letter" of July 1963.

"There is only one generally recognized procedure for maintaining an alert, up-to-date staff. This is participation in creative and original research. This research is of its own intrinsic value for the staff; it cannot always be restricted to problems suitable for participation by undergraduate students or related to undergraduate instruction, and it is often incompatible with these aims. Such research must be published in the recognized scientific literature, for the staff must be subjected to the criticism of its peers.

"The selection of the areas of research is difficult (for faculty members in smaller institutions). It must be possible to conduct the research without the facilities or organization available to large institutions, but the most useful research for the objectives of the eduational program would undoubtedly involve topics of vital current interest in the field concerned."

CHAPTER SIX

THE COLLEGE CURRICULUM AND
THE IMPORTANCE OF INTEGRATION

It is not my intention to go into the details of building a worthy college curriculum and to describe the importance of effective integration in the carrying out of the program of studies. This I shall leave for the forthcoming book, A Handbook on Administration in Catholic Institutions of Higher Education. I do, however, feel it advisable to discuss some important principles in connection with the making of a curriculum and in the case of a Catholic college the importance, if not necessity, of genuine integration in the implementation of the curriculum.

The importance of the curriculum in building a college of excellence is perhaps second only to the teacher. It is, of course, the nature of the curriculum that identifies the college. Much of the controversy over the years on the nature of the college and its program seems to have been stimulated by a national crisis of some kind, when the youth of the land in general and college graduates in particular have seemed to fail to meet, to the satisfaction of national leaders, the emergency needs of their country. For, example, much dissatisfaction was expressed by some at the apparent attitude of the American people, especially college graduates, toward the hardships imposed upon them during World War II by the exigencies of the time. The bitter grumbling about the military draft, rationing of food, and other measures enforced to preserve our resources was laid primarily at the door of the college-trained citizen. To many this generalized attitude was an indication that our educational system had failed, and the American college, as usual, was the chief scape-goat. Special investigations were inauguarated to determine the changes which were necessary to bring the American College around to a condition which would enable it to fulfill its real duty to the American people, and individual educational specialists rushed to express their own views on the situation. This series of events may almost be called a routine which coincides or follows every national upheaval of any consequence.

It should not be said, however, that these periods of general reappraisal have been totally without benefit. It is good to refresh our thinking on the philosophy of higher education and to keep these goals closely related to the needs of modern living. This does not mean necessarily the advocating of drastic changes merely for the sake of change, nor that the modern world requires a new philosophy of the curriculum and new principles of curriculum construction. On the contrary, in stating a need to refresh our thinking in the philosophy of higher education, we wish to emphasize the stabilizing quality of a worthy philosophy of education and of the educational goals which are so largely shaped by it. True, the need for the continuous evaluation of the curriculum at all educational levels is seen most frequently in terms of needed revision in order to keep up with the far-reaching changes of our times. While we would recognize this need and even emphasize it, we hold that the fundamentals of a Catholic philosophy of the curriculum and the nature of its basic goals are anchored in a true and unchanging philosophy of life based on the unchanging nature of man and his final destiny, and that the need for continuous study and revision of the curriculum lies in seeking improved means of reaching these goals in a highly unstable environment. These

"means" are commonly called the specific objectives of the college.

What has just been said concerning the nature
of the curriculum goals does not mean that any
single curriculum pattern or formula of construction
is possible or desirable. In defining the curriculum
as designed "under the immediate inspiration of
specific objectives," we allow for any number of
variations in content and approach. While there are
the general aims which all colleges, and especially
those of a single type, share in common, there are
also specific aims peculiar to the individual institution. Thus such factors as geographic location within a section of the country, its urban or rural characteristics, its size and resources, its organization
as a boarding or day college, and its predominating
religious-philosophical background (Benedictine,
Franciscan, Jesuit, Dominican, or any other) will
all have important effects. The first and most fundamental principle of curriculum construction then
is that the college's philosophy and its aims must be
worked out in specific detail and its curriculum must
be built directly on these aims.

Perhaps the next important consideration is that
of the intellectual calibre and previous training of
the youth who will enter the particular institution
for further study. The curriculum must be suitable
for these students, something that is within *their*
grasp and by which *they* can be motivated to a love

of learning for its own sake. It may be almost bla-
tant to restate here that the work of the college is
largely dependent on the general intellectual capacity of the students and on the quality of the training
received at the high school level. Yet in our fervor
to develop the ideal citizen, Catholic and American,
we often forget this obvious fact. Permit us to illustrate this point. The president of a comparatively
youthful Catholic college, excellently trained himself and an outstanding product of our educational
system, envisioned the curriculum of his college as
constructed according to the principles of a program
of concentration, centered rightfully around a solid
core of philosophy and theology. He properly
weighted the curriculum heavily with philosophy
and theology and built a faculty well trained to teach
these subjects. His was an honors program required
of *all* students. But the actual quality of the preparation for college obtained in the locale which the
college serviced was completely overlooked. Since
the geographical area was rather clearly defined, the
comparatively low level of quality would not only
have been easily discernable but the inescapable
limitations placed thereby on the curriculum would
have been readliy recognized. The ignoring of this
condition, however, led to extreme confusion: a
highly trained faculty struggling to maintain a program of studies of honors-grade with a student body
unprepared for college work of this kind and, in some

instances, needing remedial work, in spelling and simple sentence structure. Obviously, the curriculum, excellent in itself, was not appropriate for that student body.

My third principle can be expressed by the single word "comprehensive." Yet it must be understood that comprehensive here does not mean that the curriculum must cover all knowledge, an impossible scope in our present proliferation of knowledge. It does mean that it must be sufficiently broad to include the major fields of knowledge in order to give the student intellectual breadth and a general integrated background for any specialization at which he aims. The importance of integration for the effectiveness of the total program could be enlarged to book-size. Here it will have to suffice to point out that the principle of integration is generally implemented by devoting the first two years of the college program (often called the lower division) to the broadening and deepening of the student's general background, with the last two years (or upper division) being given emphasis on a selected field and ancillary subjects while carrying forward throughout the entire four years, with genuine seriousness, the study of philosophy and theology.

Any tendency to meet the principle of comprehensiveness by devoting valuable space in the curriculum to the so-called "survey" courses I believe to be a fallacious application of the principle. Probably most courses have something of the nature of a survey about them, but we have reference to the "gallop" kind of instruction, based on the old false impression that education is the process of inserting as many facts as possible on a variety of subjects within the student's mind. Such courses are at best a strenuous test of the student's memory, being usually a matter of listening to someone rush through the entire history of Western civilization or the history of music or some similar expanse of material, while resting in a state of complete passivity. Of course, information so obtained is retained in the mind very briefly and is of little or no value in attaining the intellectual ends professed for a good college education.

A single word may also be used to summarize my fourth principle: flexibility. While the total program should be geared to the general intellectual characteristics of the student body, at the same time sufficient flexibility must be maintained to allow for a shifting of this common level from year to year and to meet the range of ability that exists within any student body, no matter how carefully selected by admission procedures. Thus the curriculum should not be beyond the student; nor should it lag behind him. The worthwhile college will provide for this needed flexibility through its course offerings, and the good teacher through adjustments within the courses themselves, so that each student, within reason, is worked to the limit of his capacity.

My fifth and final principle of curriculum construction is perhaps best expressed negatively: the curriculum builder should not take a narrow view of what constitutes the college curriculum. If he excludes from his planning any consideration of the physical and human resources available to carry out the program, he is apt to meet a problem very similar to that of the college president who gives no consideration to his student body. Good teachers, good equipment, good library materials, a realistic schedule all are factors so closely related to the effectiveness of the program that overlooking any one of them may result in curriculum mediocrity.

In fact, the total setting or campus life should be viewed as a great potentiality for the development of intellectual and spiritual values as well as social ones, and, as such, will make a very substantial contribution toward attaining curriculum goals. Here the American college administrator moves between the Scylla of unrestrained pleasure (e.g. the overemphasis on athletics and all its by-products and on an excessive number of social events such as dances and parties) and the Charybdis of superficialities in great abundance (lectures of doubtful academic or spiritual value, travel in the form of visiting museums and places of general tourist interest, and a superabundance of mediocre concerts and theatrical productions). Certainly these are matters not to be condemned in themselves but to be fostered and encouraged only in a manner commensurate with their real value and with their place in the entire college plan. For proper evaluation and to avoid overexaggeration beyond their educational value, they should be viewed strictly as part of a total program, complementing and supplementing the curriculum in the attainment of the college's aims. If each is viewed as an entity, it would seem that both will suffer as effective tools in educating the "whole" student.

But no curriculum, regardless of how well it is constructed, will succeed if it is not well integrated in the Catholic sense. To say that much confusion existed and still exists in the educational circles of this age regarding the nature of academic integration is a decided under-statement. In our own time the term has been used often and usually very loosely, and there is frequently a complete lack of agreement both regarding its basic definition and its practical application. It has been used synonymously with "correlation" and "fusion" and other such terms. To avoid adding to this over-all confusion, I wish first to narrow the concept of integration as relating directly to the student, as a "dynamic process, which may be described as a conscious effort on the part of the individual to reestablish an equilibrium in his relationships to the sources of learning." [1] Thus I would prefer to speak of "correlation" with life and the "correlation" or "fusion" of subject fields and of an integrating curriculum. At the same time, however, I would broaden the concept of integration as being synonymous with "synthesis" or "unity" within the intellectual life of the individual, the perfecting of the whole man for the attainment of his ultimate ends through the ability to think and to act properly and intelligently under varying conditions. Thus my concept of integration parallels our concept of a true education or the training of the "perfect Christian."

In discussing integration as it has been commonly used in the educational circles of our time, I must, at least for the moment, revert to a definition which I feel is only one aspect of academic integration, the so-called integration of the curriculum and course content with life. The quality of teaching in an educational institution is often severely criticized today on the ground that it is lacking in this kind of integration. The work of teachers in an entire field of study, as, for example, Latin studies during the first quarter of this century, has been so condemned. The subject, it was said, was being taught in a vacuum. Indeed, in the case of Latin the teachers were frequently and openly accused of directly

[1] Rev. Joseph A. Gorham, "Curriculum Organzation and Construction," in the Curriculum of the Catholic Secondary School, ed. Rev. Michael J. McKeough, O. Praem., Washington, 1945.

causing the decline of interest in Latin on the part of contemporary youth because they ignored any kind of integration with modern living. A certain United States Commissioner of Education, as long as he was in office, persistently belabored public school education, and private education as well, for its failure to train youth for life. And even more recently, teachers of mathematics, especially in the high school, were asked in no uncertain terms by educational leaders to cease teaching their subject as if it had no connection with anything else in the world and to "integrate" it both horizontally and vertically.

When the teachers of an educational institution as a group fail to "integrate" as they teach, they presumably teach with no thought of making the knowledge thus imparted of any direct value in the lives of their students. They teach their respective subjects solely for the sake of the subjects themselves; they are subject-centered, not student-centered. It is not surprising then that a United States Commissioner of Education became greatly concerned with such a serious weakness and went to what seems to some of us, as Catholic educators, to an opposite extreme, the reform of all public school education around a core of vocational subjects. Preparation for life through formal education was viewed in the most practical and functional way.

All this is, of course, illustrative of a kind of integration with which we would be willing to agree within reasonable limits. Certainly in the teaching of Latin those elements that relate to our own language and the various influences of Latin culture on our own contemporary civilization should be carefully and frequently pointed out. And teachers of mathematics should avoid purely theoretical problems such as those involving the speed of a hare and a turtle or the distribution of a small plot of land which, after its division, would not provide sufficient space upon which to place the very smallest of buildings. Most of us would be willing to assert that, in due proportion, integration with life is necessary for good teaching in any field. But it is at this point that the secular and Catholic educator come to the parting of the ways.

The secular educator is quite satisfied with a fair amount of success in achieving integration with life and would probably seek no further integration, if indeed he is aware of the existence or desirability of any other. The true Catholic educator cannot be satisfied with this alone. Indeed, if he stops here, his educational institution will be little different from the secular He must seek integration through theology, under whatever name theology may raise her head in a Catholic school or college. In other words, the Catholic teacher must seek integration with the life of the next world as well as with life in the present, since the two are integrally related, and are one.

The following is a recent statement and quite appropriate at this stage of our discussion:

"Truth, no doubt, has unity, and man in his striving for knowledge and truth is driven by a desire for synthesis and unity. Truth and unity, says St. Thomas, are two interchangeable concepts. For to understand, to comprehend, means to discover interconnection and order, to reduce multiple data to a unity of order.

"But this unity of the truth which always remains more an ideal of man than an achieved result, must not make us forget the multiplicity of diverse levels or realms of truth. For instance, we may distinguish the truth of the every-day practical world, the truth of modern positive science, the truth pursued by philosophy and the truth we attain and cherish as religious faith" [1]

This concept of integration, based on the acceptance of the fact that all knowledge is a single unit and that it can only be a unit if there is a central, unifying force, is no twentieth century idea. St. Augustine said:

"There is an immutable truth embracing all things that are true; a truth you cannot call yours,

[1] Albert Dondayne, Faith and the World, Duquesne Studies: Theological Series, I. Pittsburgh, Pa.,: Duquesne University Press, 1963. p. 181.

or mine, or any man's, but which is present to all
and gives itself to all who discern the things that
are immutably true, as a light which in some mirac-
ulous way is both secret and yet open to all." [1]
St. Thomas also speaks often of the "oneness of
truth" and of man's unified nature, so that the process of true learning requires an integrating and
ordered relationship among the various disciplines,
all subordinated to man's ultimate end. The Catholic educator has always recognized this basic unity
of knowledge and the need for synthesis in a Christian education, and he has been blessed with the
only existing successful means of integration by
reason of his unhesitating confidence in the truths
of the theology and philosophy which he professes.
Many non-Catholics envy us this priceless possession; many of them also would gladly adopt our
theology and philosophy for the purpose at least of
achieving the integration and unity in their teaching which is so necessary if the educational product
is to be the integrated man. Because they may not
use the name of God in the classroom and may not
use principles of thinking to which sectarian significance may be attached, they must confine themselves to a social philosophy involving only the
affairs of this world.

[1] St. Augustine, De libero arbitrio, 2. 12. 33.

To implement successfully the Catholic concept of integration, more is needed than the mere introduction into the classroom of courses in theology or religion, philosophy, and Church history, important as these contributions are to the student's over-all education. The ultimate objectives of these courses and the ultimate objective of the total program must penetrate every teaching field of the school or college. Courses in theology, philosophy, and to a much less extent history contain the tangible material by which the unification of all other fields may be brought about. Thus, these basic subjects, in addition to their own intrinsic value, must seep through all other subjects and serve as the pivotal and unifying factors of Catholic education. I do not hesitate to say that thus far in the United States this has not been done very successfully. This is the great challenge to Catholic educators in general today.

In recent years we think it may be said that some success has been achieved by Catholics in the teaching of theology, philosophy, and Church history, and while much still remains to be done in these fields, far less progress has been made in the actual integration of the other subjects of the college curriculum. The cause is perhaps twofold: inadequacies in the organization of the curriculum and in the training of the teachers themselves. I have already discussed both factors in previous chapters, emphasizing the synthesizing aspects of the program of concentration as an improved organizational device over the traditional major-minor plan.[1] Certainly a poorly organized curriculum which gives each and every field of knowledge a discrete status and nothing more is not likely to produce the integrated college graduate, but the best efforts of a well-trained faculty can counteract and overcome many of the difficulties imposed by such a curriculum. On the other hand, the best curriculum, organized for inter-departmental cooperation and correlation, will do little to promote the attainment of an integrated education if faculty members are unable to correlate their subjects with Catholic theology and philosophy, because of lack of training or because they recognize no personal responsibility in the matter. For this reason, I feel that the training of the college teacher is the most important single factor in bringing about good Catholic integration.

It is not uncommon for a teacher, even a religious, to state openly that he is a teacher of science or any other secular subject but not of religion. In the technical or literal sense this is true, but if the philosophical implications for him as a teacher of science in a Catholic educational institution are not recognized, then his students are no better off in

[1] Cf. Handbook on Administration in Catholic Institutions of Higher Education, by Deferrari and Watrin, Boston, in press.

their learning of the sciences than if they had attended secular institutions. The very rationale of Catholic education is thus being attacked. I do not mean to imply in any way, however, that we would substitute preaching or the teaching of theological content *per se* in the science laboratory or the Latin classroom. This is not proper theological integration. The teacher of chemistry and the teacher of Latin are first of all teachers of their respective subjects, and it is through the content of their particular fields that they hope to attain within their students certain well-defined objectives pertaining directly to their fields. These objectives, however, have a close relationship to the over-all college objectives, which, in a Catholic college, have evolved from Catholic philosophical and educational principles. The contribution of each teacher consists in the implementing of these objectives and these principles in a practical way through the teaching of his fields. To disregard the Christian entirely in favor of the scientist is completely preposterous in Catholic education. But to disregard the scientist in favor of the Christian can be carried to an extreme and falls far short of true integration, since it is obvious that the over-emphasis of theological content to the de-emphasis of the science content is simply the reversing of emphases and not the unification of both contents toward the common objectives of Christian education. A modicum of common sense should

5. *Higher Cath. Ed.*

keep the teacher on an even keel in this matter. For those who have any qualms of conscience in this regard or desire further clarification I would recommend a careful reading of Gilson's *"The Intelligence in the Service of Christ the King"* concerning the makings of a Christian savant, philosopher, or artist, and Cardinal Newman's *"Idea of a University"* for his eloquent discussion of the inter-relationships of the disciplines, theology among and above the others. In fact, Cardinal Newman's work is basic reading for all in any study of the problems of Catholic college integration. As Father Benard has pointed out: "A study of Newman's complete writings on education does give us valuable clues as to the proper integration of Catholic education which achieves a *unity* of intellectual and moral influence through: First, the spirit and atmosphere of a Catholic institution of learning, obeying and fostering Catholic dogma and guided by the authoritative voice of the Church; and second, through the teachers in a Catholic institution of learning, who unite in themselves and hence promote in their students both learning and devotion. This does not mean, however, that a teacher should substitute moralizing and preaching for a sound and scientific presentation of the subject." [1] It seems appropriate then to conclude our

---

[1] Rev. Edmon D. Benard, "Theology as Pivotal: Newman's Views, "*in* Integration in Catholic Colleges and Universities, ed. Roy J. Deferrari, Washington, D.C., 1950.

discussion of the role of teacher in the integration process with the words of Cardinal Newman in which he describes the Catholic teacher simply as the product of a truly Catholic education, one who is a "Catholic speaking as a Catholic spontaneously will speak, on the classics, or fine arts, or poetry, or whatever else he has taken in hand." [2]

[1] John Henry Cardinal Newman, *The Idea of a University*, New York, 1959, p. 286.

CHAPTER SEVEN

GRADUATE STUDY IN PRIMARILY
UNDERGRADUATE INSTITUTIONS

A brief definition of graduate study is appropriate here. It is not merely a program of studies beyond the bachelor's degree. It is advanced work, of course, and presupposes a thorough basic knowledge of the chief field of study, commonly known as the "major," and a similar experience, although not necessarily as intensive, in one or more ancillary fields, usually called the "minor" or "minors."

I am concerned here strictly with the advisability of a college of simple organization offering work leading to the master's degree in the traditional sense, as a preparation for research. The objectives of the general college, especially as defined for some of the more recent bachelor's programs, such as the so-called program of concentration, may have certain aims in common with those of the master's degree, and thus the advisability of the college offering such curriculums may with some reason be considered. The usual college of simple organization, however, should under no circumstances attempt to offer a plan of studies leading to the doctorate, because such a program has very specific objectives quite distinct from the main purpose of the general college and requires resources far beyond those usually available in the college.

The following are some considerations which the administration of a college should bear in mind, if they are inclined to offer studies leading to the master's degree.

I. *Basic Principles*

1. The primary objective of a college is, of course, a strong undergraduate program both of studies and appropriate collegiate activities. Until the college authorities feel that all major problems connected with the support of such a program have been solved, they should not think of installing a graduate curriculum of any kind. From the very nature of a college, problems will always be present. It is only when administrators feel that they have the resources available to meet these satisfactorily and still have the means of setting up at least a limited program of graduate studies, should they ever

think of taking such a step. Any evidence that such a venture, however circumscribed, is detracting support to any degree important for the college as such is very damaging for the institution as a whole. Educational leaders of the region and of the country at large will have little confidence in the administration of such an institution.

2. The financial cost of launching and supporting a graduate program should be carefully weighed. Graduate work properly carried on involves small classes and a very highly trained faculty, all of which is extremely costly. Any thought that graduate studies will attract a sufficient number of students to support themselves even approximately is a pure delusion. As a matter of fact, the larger the the graduate student body becomes, granted that it will be properly provided for, the greater will be the financial deficit.

3. A fifth year of undergraduate work leading to the master's degree is obviously graduate work only in name. It may be called for chronological reasons post-graduate work but by reason of its nature cannot be said to be graduate. A so-called "fifth year" of college work leading to a certificate, as practiced in some colleges, is another matter and may be very worth while, but granting a graduate degree for such a year of study is palpably improper and very damaging to the academic reputation of the college.

4. What kind of master's degree should be given by an institution devoted essentially exclusively to general education on the undergraduate level? I personally feel that there is only one kind of master's degree worthy of consideration for any purpose and by any kind of institution. This is the traditional master's degree which requires an expanded training in the content of one main field and possibly of a minor field, but always from the research point of view. The approach used in the courses involved will train the candidate in the use of handbooks of the field, in gathering and organizing material, and in the critical evaluation of such material and of any work of scholarship. The program may well be crowned by a limited piece of independent research. This kind of training will serve best the future teacher and the future members of the professions.

Any such programs as those specifically designed for teachers, where the degree granted is termed a master's degree for teachers, are in many instances devices to make the work involved easy. This is done by eliminating the usual requirements of a dissertation, the experience of reading professional literature in a foreign language, the comprehensive examination, and others. Thus the very purpose of the degree is defeated.

II. *Organization*

(1) Since we are talking here of possible graduate work within a college, it must somehow be fitted into the organizational framework of the college without damaging the structure of the college. After all, the college and its work are paramount and whatever graduate work is undertaken definitely subsidiary. The university organization of largely independent schools should be avoided. Graduate work should not be set up as a separate school or in any way that will make it sharply distinguished from the college. It may well be established as a division with a director and an advisory council made up of the heads of departments offering graduate work, but the director should be subject to the dean of the college, just as the dean is subject to the president. It is assumed, of course, that the college will be quite sympathetic with the division of graduate studies and will work in harmony with its director. Unless this be so, the college will be torn by conflicting views, and it will not profit as it should from such a program.

(2) The teachers in the graduate division should have the degree of doctor or the master's degree with a number of courses beyond the masterate toward the doctorate. It goes without saying that this training should be obtained from departments of high graduate calibre. This statement needs to be made

because of the large number of master's degrees of little value which are granted annually throughout the land.

(3) The program of studies leading to the master's degree should have about two-thirds of its courses in the so-called major field and one-third in the minor field. If the subjects of study are in closely allied areas, some liberality may be exercised in determining the exact amount of work to be accomplished in the major and minor fields.

(4) Some graduate courses may be open to undergraduate seniors; rarely, if ever, to others. This would assume that the undergraduates concerned would be able to take their places alongside the graduate students and would fulfill the usual requirements of the graduate courses. They should not be given preferential treatment by reason of their being undergraduates.

(5) While a good college library is very helpful for graduate work, the collection of books must be strengthened to meet the more specialized nature of the graduate courses. This is especially true of periodical literature. Current subscriptions and back numbers of scholarly journals in both English and foreign languages, and for both the members of the graduate faculty and the students should be provided.

(6) If the graduate students reach any appreciable number, problems of social life are bound to

arise. It cannot be expected that the graduate student, while endeavoring to adapt himself to the graduate point of view in both the classroom and in his private study, will go along contentedly and advantageously with the social life of the undergraduate. The deans of men and women can, without undue difficulty, work out a satisfactory way of life for the graduate student, and this should be done. Perhaps, even of greater importance is to have a faculty which under prevailing undergraduate conditions can adapt itself to the graduate approach in the classroom.

III. *Advantages*

Carefully planned and carried out, graduate studies in undergraduate institutions have some distinct advantages for the college as a whole.

(1) The library of the college will of necessity take on additional strength and greater usefulness for the undergraduate, as graduate courses require a richer collection of reference works and supplementary reading.

(2) The graduate courses open to properly qualified undergraduates will offer additional advantages and a greater challenge to undergraduates. An important means for solving the problem of caring for the superior student will be at hand.

(3) The college may well be able by certain special graduate programs to furnish a distinct service to the region in which it is located. In this way

it will increase in the minds of the people in the area a feeling of responsibility for the welfare of the institution. The bond of good will between the two will be made stronger. It has been very well said that no institution of higher education can truly prosper unless it lays its roots deeply in the region of its location.

(4) If the college is conducted by a religious community, the problem of the higher training of the members of the religious group will become much easier for the superiors. The training itself, within a restricted academic area, may well be at least of a calibre equal for the most part to that obtained in a large university. This, of course, is predicated on the belief that religious superiors, thinking of the general welfare of the community, wishing to promote the intellectual interests, will be willing to develop the library and strengthen the faculty for this purpose. Mention should also be made of the greater intellectual resources made available for the members of the community at large, including those not necessarily engaged in work toward a degree.

CHAPTER EIGHT

DISCIPLINE IN CATHOLIC INSTITUTIONS
OF HIGHER EDUCATION

The purposes or aims of an educational institution are of basic importance to every phase and aspect of its organization and administration. To these purposes all educational policies, activities, and functions of the institution must relate: curriculums, faculty training, extra-curricular activities, library development, graduation requirements, and others. By the same token no activity should be carried on by any institution which is not related to its general and specific objectives. Because of this all-encompassing relationship, it is of paramount importance that a written statement of purposes be formulated for each institution of higher education and that this statement reflect, by its conciseness, its clarity, and its excellence of phraseology, the results of a thorough and comprehensive study of the very reason for that institution's existence. This statement, moreover, may be regarded as a description of the factors which determine the disciplinary nature of the college or university.

Since every phase of higher education within a college or university should directly or, at least indirectly, contribute to the attainment of the stated purposes, any worth while evaluation of any part of the higher education process will revolve around the institution's objectives. In fact, the evaluation of an academic institution might be defined as an effort to determine how well and to what extent the institution as a whole or its component parts are attaining its purposes. Thus in a good institution of higher education, where informal self-evaluation is both continuous and constant, its stated purposes are not only used as valuable criteria to guide and control but they themselves are from time to time reviewed and weighed in the light of current needs and resources.

However, equally as important as the existence of a satisfactory and comprehensive statement of purposes is the widespread dissemination and understanding of the purposes among the administrators, the members of the faculty, and the students of the college or university. The extent to which these purposes are attained will depend greatly on the ability and the willingness of all concerned to work toward the one common goal with all the power of a well organized disciplinary effort. Certainly, without personal knowledge and understanding of the goal, no true unity of effort can be hoped for, and the resulting lack of discipline cannot help but be reflected in the final outcomes. Therefore, instead of merely relegating the statement of purposes to an infrequently used page of the college catalogue, it should appear conspicuously in other official documents and handbooks, both for faculty and student use; it should be clarified and explained during freshman orientation week; it should be referred to frequently and discussed on every possible occasion; it should have a fitting place in faculty meetings and in student organizations, assemblies and convocations, until even the least inspired instructor and the most disinterested student must finally be made aware of what the college or university is trying to do. It can be hoped, from such a starting point as this, that the development, implementation, and explanation of policies, procedures, and regulations will be assisted and accepted by both faculty and students with greater understanding, sympathy, and cooperation, and thus that better discipline will be maintained.

Because of its importance, then, in shaping and implementing policies and in evaluating outcomes, the official statement of purposes or of the institution's disciplinary concepts should be drawn up or revised with great care. It is not the job of any one administrator, but rather should be the result of a cooperative study by a committee representative of both the administration and the faculty. The study made by such a committee should be sufficiently comprehensive to include not only the accepted and sound principles of Catholic educational philosophy but also those additional factors which will have direct bearing on the particular institution: the immediate locale and community, the kind (men, women, or both), and level (intellectual, economic, social), of the student it will service, the needs of modern youth and society in general, and the physical and intellectual resources of the religious community concerned. In other words, a serious effort should be made to draw up a statement of purposes that is both realistic and practical, one which shows an awareness of current and actual needs and is attainable in its every respect.

The following is a statement of the purpose of a Catholic college for men, which, as will be seen, embodies the basis of the institution's disciplinary life.

"XX College exists for the students and offers to them the opportunity for self-realization. Education is the process by which it is accomplished. Liberal education is the process by which it is best accomplished, because liberal education looks to the development of the whole man and of all his faculties.

"Education is primarily directed to the disciplining and development of the mind. To open the student's mind to the whole realm of truth, to enligthen and strengthen his reason, to develop as fully as possible his powers to think, is specifically the work of the College. Nothing is allowed to detract from this essential aim.

"Education as a process of growth is not complete, however, and is ineffective, unless mental discipline and development are accompanied by the development of virtue and good character. A Catholic institution would indeed find it difficult to justify its existence, if it did not strive to permeate all its activity with the spirit of Christ and with the ideals of conduct and religious life which are found in His teaching. In striving for the development of virtue and good character in the students, furthermore, the College is carrying on the highest traditions of a liberal education. True liberal education has always sought the formation not only of the intelligent man, but of the good man.

"The College also believes that liberal education has never been and should not be divorced from the practical needs of life. The 'ivory tower' concept of education for leisure is not realistic in twentieth century America. Since most of our students do not belong to the leisure class, they are understandably interested in securing some kind of gainful occupation soon after their graduation, unless they go on to professional studies. This is a reasonable objective, but the whole concept of liberal education and indeed the purpose of life itself can be vitiated and made meaningless, if material gain is made the primary aim.

"Students, in their impatience and eagerness to become vocationally competent, are inclined to take the view that the shortest path is the best. They become restless under the disciplines which are called 'humanistic,' unless they can be made to understand that, in the long range view, such studies are of great importance even for vocational plans. They must be made to see that where technical competence is without direction and without firm anchorage in fundamental principles, accumulation of wealth is paralleled by the decay of men.

"Sound vocational education should be based upon broad foundations of knowledge. Ways of speaking and writing, the ability to get at once to the heart of a problem found in a book, a report, or an analysis, knowledge of human motivation, knowledge of oneself and others, are necessary for promotions and advancements in business. But no one can develop these abilities or acquire this knowledge in a few weeks or a few months. Psychology, theology, philosophy, economics, literature, history are the sources which have to be tapped.

"Experience teaches that development of the student's intellectual capacities by the discipline of the liberal arts and sciences is the very best way of preparing him for the practical life. Specialized training for specific occupations may be required, but it will be made easier, quicker, more lasting, and more productive when founded upon the disciplines of a liberal education. To become a resourceful person, alert and responsive to varying demands, trained for all sorts of jobs in general and perhaps for one field in particular, requires a preparation and a point of view which come only from deep and careful self-cultivation. These facts are becoming more and more clearly recognized by medical and dental schools, by law schools, by schools of engineering, by business corporations, and even by the directors of military training schools.

"We may summarize the aims of XX College as follows: (1) To develop the student's mind. This is the primary aim. (2) To foster the development of virtue and good character in the student by every means possible. (3) To prepare the student in a general way for life's work and to advise him on his vocational plans."

All of the ideas mentioned above are in the last analysis strictly matters of discipline in the general sense of the term. The entire plan of a single institution of higher education for the achievement of its purposes in the most effective way possible is nothing more than a gravely conceived plan of discipline.

The ordinary meaning of discipline in institutions of higher education as understood by the average person is, of course, the making and enforcement of regulations that will preserve the peace and decorum of the total institution. It has been said with some basis in fact that the higher are the academic standards of a college, the better are the standards of everyday conduct. If a college requires any great number of regulations to enable it to keep ordinary peaceful living on its campus, serious academic short-comings should be looked for.

An important academic axiom is that every hour in the college classroom should be backed by at least two hours of private study. Closely allied to this is the belief of many successful educators that the good teacher and the good institution will develop in students a desire for independent study and great success at it. All this, of course, indicates praise-worthy maturity.

There are, however, many harmful and superficial axioms and notions current among the people and even among some educators, some of which should be mentioned here. The thought that colleges are primarily concerned with intellectual training is far too little known even in places where it should be of primary consideration. Coming to my office a little earlier than usual one morning I met the mother of a young lady who was a member of my beginning Greek class. She was a very good student, or at least had the potentiality for being one. Her otherwise good performance in class was punctuated with all too many instances of being quite unprepared. I spoke of this to her mother, expecting to receive some cooperation in remedying the situation, but she very confidently, as if pronouncing a great educational truth, replied: "Well, I want my daughter to be an all-round girl!" In other words, in the mother's mind and this, of course, had been transmitted to the daughter, to devote herself to attaining high accomplishment in scholarship brings lack of balance in one's general development! An intensive intellectual development need not, of course, result in a "dull" girl. Is it too much to expect that students may have fruitful contacts with teachers, visitors from other institutions, as well as fellow students, with whom they may discuss their special fields of interest and common problems as well as problems connected with the world?

Some social activities worthy of a good college are an active and intelligent life of worship on the campus, reflecting the best thought on the matter in the Church today; athletics, music, and art on a limited scale for sheer recreation, with some guidance from those specializing in the fields so that these become learning experiences also, even while being recreational; some trips into the neighboring area of the college with a good purpose, apostolic and informational as well as social. The experience of student government, if not too time-consuming, may be beneficial. Intercollegiate groups may also be helpful, since it is good to mingle with non-Catholics, but all this can become a great distraction. There seems to have developed of late a growth in the number of student periodicals in the fundamental fields of study such as chemistry. This seems excellent for the encouragement of independent thinking and writing. But students who date frequently during the week and over Friday, Saturday, and Sunday of a week-end, and take time out to travel considerable distances for week-end dates, would, it seems to me, ordinarily flunk out of any worthwhile college. The practice of hazing is regularly placed in the category of worthwhile social events, and many arguments are brought forth to defend it in this place. This phase of student life, long since stamped out by the authorities of truly serious institutions or departed to a peaceful rest because of the growing apathy of the students and others concerned, is a distressing sign of immaturity and naïveté.

Good discipline, as we have attempted to describe it above, should lead to the habits of a well-balanced life. Catholic colleges which carry on their work with their purpose constantly in the minds of administrators, teachers, and students should yield very well disciplined graduates prepared to meet the responsibilities placed upon them by Church and country.

CHAPTER NINE

FACULTY PARTICIPATION IN
THE LIFE OF AN INSTITUTION

That the members of the faculty of an academic institution may perform fully their appropriate duties in a college or university, they must be made to feel at home within its confines. They must not be made to feel that they should be content just so long as they receive their salaries regularly in return for performing their teaching duties faithfully like a group of hired hands. Their activities and their thinking should extend far beyond that. They are a part of a composite force of human beings—priests, nuns, lay women, and lay men, all of whom as a unit, working harmoniously together, make the institution of higher education live and develop. In organizing a college or a university it is comparatively easy to describe the duties of the faculty in the institution's statutes or constitution, but the good will and the active cooperation of the members of the faculty requires the support, the stimulus, and the active interest of the highest authorities of the institution, the president and the board of trustees.

The support of the highest authorities of the college or university must take a practical form. The members of the faculty must feel that every effort is being made on the part of the authorities of the institution to give them a comfortable living wage. They have a right to expect to find reliable provisions for retirement and pension. Any institution of higher education that pretends to any respectability in the educational world of the United States recognizes these responsibilities, and it must be said that some Catholic instittuions have lived up to their responsibilities in these matters with increasing fidelity.

The administrators of Catholic institutions have until comparatively recently not always understood the nature of sabbatical leaves. I recall vividly when as Dean of the Graduate School of Arts and Sciences of The Catholic University of America I inquired of the then Rector whether any provision had been made regarding sabbatical leaves receiving an indignant reply as follows: "I never take a long vacation!" Indeed, the president of one of our largest

Catholic universities openly proclaims in this day and age that he will have no truck with them. In the beginning sabbatical leaves in such institutions as regularly granted them were regarded as years off with pay granted every seventh year of service to regular full-time members of the teaching staff. The following statement represents fairly well the nature and understanding of sabbatical leaves prevalent in institutions of higher education in the United States, Catholic and non-Catholic.

"Sabbatical leaves are understood as leaves of absence with pay, granted to faculty members in recognition of service to the institution and of scholarly contributions and to provide opportunity for scholarly development. It is understood that such leaves are not intended for purposes of recreation or recuperation.

"Professors, associate professors, and assistant professors are eligible for sabbatical leave after at least six years of service in professorial rank.

"Regular sabbatical leaves are not guaranteed. Sabbatical leaves may be granted only when ab- absence will not seriously impair the interests of the institution.

"Sabbatical leaves, if granted, will provide full salary for two semesters. This is given with the understanding that the faculty member is not receiving compensation for services at another institution."

A very delicate matter in the relationship of authorities of an institution and the members of a faculty is that of tenure. This is especially true of Catholic colleges and universities. The abuses in this respect have been many and in some cases harrowing. Within the year a startling case has been called to my attention within a very well-known Catholic college for women. A man with a large family served on the faculty for nearly ten years. He waited patiently during that time for a reliable statement as to his tenure so that he might purchase a home in the neighborhood of the college, hoping to make his position a life-time career. With an advance notice of only three months, he was informed that his services would not be needed for the next academic year. To be sure, there are many occasions when a Catholic religious community conducting an institution of higher education, needs a teacher for only a year or two while a member of the religious group is being prepared to do the work. In such instances the situation should be explained in detail to the person chosen for the job. In every case, a notice of dismissal should be given at least one full academic year in advance. Of course, all provisions established in the statutes of the college relative to dismissal should be scrupulously observed.

Another subject of great gravity in connection with the contacts of the faculty members with the institutional authorities is so-called academic freedom. Some years ago, before World War II, the subject of academic freedom was a slightly difficult one for Catholic educators to discuss with their non-Catholic colleagues, because of the extreme attitude taken at that time by non-sectarian educators on this subject. I myself at a meeting of the Association of American Colleges heard the president [1] of one of the leading universities of the country say before a large audience of educators that he did not see how any institution could say that it possessed academic freedom unless it permitted the members of the teaching staff to say anything whatever that they pleased. Much has happened in relation to this problem since then to make educators take a very different stand, especially the infiltration in all walks of American life of Communists and Communistic thought. Catholic and non-Catholic educators alike are very much in agreement with the following basic principle: Members of the faculty may speak freely on subjects within their field, provided they say nothing contrary to the professed philosophy and theology of the institution and nothing subversive of the national government. This statement in some similar form appears regularly in statutes and material submitted by institutions in answer to the usual questionnaire.

[1] He is now retired but very much before the public eye publishing on academic and political affairs.

Such a published principle seems like an easy solution to a difficult problem, and it is so, provided an academic president and boards of trustees have the character and the strength of mind to uphold it strongly. But unfortunately, when men have strong personal views and even secret ambitions which are contravened even quite unwittingly by members of the teaching staff either within or outside the classroom, they will often react in a manner quite unbecoming to a reputable center of learning and directly opposed to the simple principle expressed above. Moreover, such action will do the institution great harm. Neither the general public nor the individuals and foundations interested in supporting institutions of learning will have any confidence in it. Within the institution itself the morale of the members of the faculty and of all those interested in it in any way will be shattered.

For sources of information on current thinking and practice regarding freedom of teaching on the university and college level, [1] I refer to four documents of The Catholic University of America. These clearly define and explain the basic principles and statements of implementation on the nature and importance and also the practical reality of academic freedom.

[1] For the content of the next three pages I have drawn heavily on Dr. George F. Donovan's article in the Catholic University of America Affiliation Bulletin for Institutions of Higher Education, Series XIX, No. 2, entitled: Academic Freedom: A Reappraisal.

The four publications are: an unpublished statement entitled, Freedom of Teaching and Research, The Catholic University of America Announcements; A Manual for Faculty Promotions and Appointments at The Catholic University of America; and A Statement of Objectives of The Catholic University of America Chapter of the American Association of University Professors.

The first of these sources is a statement prepared by University authorities recently, designed to express briefly and definitely the status of the institution on the question of freedom in the classroom.

"Briefly, the purpose of any true university is to recognize truth when it meets it, to broaden the confines of existing truth, and finally, as a necessary climax to these two, to spread the knowledge of this truth, while at the same time, instilling into the minds of men a proper understanding of how to use this knowledge.

"The Catholic University of America recognizes truth as positive and unchangeable. There can be no contradictions within its sphere. Truth concerns all fields of knowledge, and there can be no contradiction between truth in one field and truth in another.

"A member of the teaching staff may not teach as true what he knows to be false or teach as a fact or as a universal law what is yet but hypothesis or theory. He may, if he wishes, express his own opinions, but they must be declared such and not facts. He may not teach anything contradictory to established truth, whether this truth be definitely known of itself or from unquestioned human authority, or from the Catholic Church speaking within its lawful sphere. Obviously within this scope, no one may teach anything injurious to the welfare of the United States of America." [1]

Besides the University memorandum, which has just been consulted, is the more brief and better known source of information, the Announcements of the University. [2] In describing the purpose of the University's Graduate School of Arts and Sciences the statement declares:

"The Graduate School of The Catholic University of America has always served a double purpose. It has fostered the discovery of knowledge and has, in an ever widening range, concerned itself with the imparting of knowledge.... For the ever expanding mechanism of Catholic higher education it aims to train teachers and administrators and research specialists in the proven ways of scholarship, enabling them to pass on to others the accumulated treasures of knowledge by their own researches ac-

[1] Freedom of Teaching and Research, Memorandum 1956, The Catholic University of America, typewritten statement.

[2] The Catholic University of America Announcements. The Graduate School of Arts and Sciences, The School of Social Science, Graduate Studies in the School of Engineering and Architecture: 1956-1957. Washington, D.C.

cording as bent and opportunity allow. It brings to American research, particularly in that part of our heritage which is Catholic in origin and circumstances, the insight and viewpoint that comes only from life within the Church."

In the quotation teaching and research are considered on the graduate school level, yet the basic values behind teaching described therein are not different from instruction in other university and college fields. Although there is no direct reference to freedom of teaching, there is, nevertheless, a list of aims which suggest in no uncertain language, the University's interest in, and endorsement of those conditions which produce freedom in teaching and research.

A third source is the University *Manual for Faculty Promotions and Appointments*. Herein [1] are described in a statement concerned with the University's aims as related to research three important purposes.

"The aim of The Catholic University of America is to search out truth scientifically, to safeguard it, and to apply it to moulding and shaping of both private and public life."

In this simple but basic statement the University repeats its belief in the concept of freedom of teaching. Its first purpose, to look for truth scien-

[1] A Manual for Faculty Promotions and Appointments at The Catholic University of America. Washington D.C. 1956, p. 6.

tifically, clearly implies that the scholar will be free to search for knowledge on a scientific basis which is in itself a genuinely free method. The second aim, to safeguard true knowledge, presupposes competent teachers who are free to defend and preserve the truth. The third purpose, to apply truth to the private and public life of the nation, presumes that the faculty members are qualified to understand and use truth for the good of their fellowmen, their country, and their Church.

The fourth and final document to be considered here is the short pamphlet on the aims of the local chapter of the American Association of University Professors. The passages quoted here and the comments therein are as follows:

"The C.U.A. Chapter of the American Association of University Professors is established as a free, autonomous association of scholars to promote the interests of its members, and of the faculty as a whole and in doing so to promote the well-being of the entire University community."

Under the title of objectives, one of which is the promotion of the professional life of its members and of the faculty, are listed four means as follows:

1. "By providing the opportunity for free and independent discussion of common interests and problems of the most appropriate means for dealing with these effectively.

2. "By sponsoring studies and making information available concerning the status of university professors in this and other institutions, in matters such as salaries, tenure, promotion, sabbatical leaves, a voice in university affairs, etc.

3. "By making representation through appropriate channels in the interests of the faculty as occasion suggests.

4. "By maintaining communication and by cooperating with professors of other universities to promote common interests through the regional and national ogranization of the A.A.U.P."

The second purpose of the chapter is concerned with the stimulation of high standards of scholarship and professional competence. Another section working together with similar groups,

"by cooperating with other chapters in the region to promote academic discussion and the interchange of ideas between members of the faculty of this university and those of other universities in the region."

It must be said, however that there is relatively little definitively defined truth in the Church. The Church encourages scholarship and expects differences of opinion in all scholarly studies including theology. Furthermore, it believes that there should be freedom here to write and to publish and to face the criticisms of other scholars.

Still another matter of grave importance in connection with administration-faculty relationships is the granting to the faculty of some voice in the institution's general affairs. This is mentioned above as an important objective of the local chapter of the A.A.U.P. Moreover, scarcely a single questionnaire from an accrediting agency of any importance fails to inquire about the extent of the faculty's participation in the administration of the institution. This is an extremely delicate matter. I have not infrequently heard administrators ask with indignation, if not heat, "What do members of the faculty know about administration? They have had no experience in it." But if properly directed, faculty participation can be extremely helpful. For one thing, they are much closer to both student and even public opinion on matters pertaining to the institution's administration, and can give advice that may well avert embarrassment and even damage to the college or university in its public relations. Of course, this participation should be in the nature of consultation and advice, and never associated with power and decision.

On the other hand, very little is said about the responsibilities of members of the faculty in return for the privileges and advantages mentioned above. In fact there are many abuses here on the part of the teaching staff. For example, the faculty member rightly demands a contract for one or more years, but in fact this is no contract at all since the faculty member rarely, if ever, considers himself bound by it. If the teacher, still under contract, receives an offer of a more attractive position from another institution, he may, of course, ask his institution's president to release him from his part of the contract, but if the president should be so ill-advised as to refuse, the teacher can depart anyway with complete impunity. No academic president will attempt to hold a teacher to his contract under such circumstances, because of the nuisance problem which the teacher can make of himself. Ethically, the teacher has an obligation and he should make every effort to live up to it or to adjust it to the satisfaction of all concerned.

The teacher also, when speaking in public, should make it very clear that he is speaking for himself alone and does not present the opinion of his institution's administration. Even when he does so, some of his listeners will insist that he speaks as a representative of his college or university. Thus it behooves him to watch over his public remarks, whether oral or written, so that they may not cause embarrassment to his institution.

He should of course, be very meticulous about preparing for his classes. He should keep conversant with the current literature and advances in his field, and assimilate this material in the lectures of his classes.

He should be prompt in fulfilling the technical requirements of his courses such as cooperating fully with the librarian with respect to the use of books and purchase of books, and in reporting promptly on the grades earned in his classes.

A good teacher will grade the academic achievement of his students with great care, because the quality of his teaching will depend heavily on his success here, and a job well done in this respect will redound greatly to the good repute of his institution. [1]

Accordingly, if a Catholic institution is to attain the full benefit of a composite group, made up of priests, nuns, laywomen, and laymen, working together for the college or university's highest good, it must have worked out a careful plan showing the responsibilities of all concerned, especially the members of the faculty, in relation to one another.

[1] See Handbook

CHAPTER TEN

BARGAIN TEACHERS IN
CATHOLIC HIGHER EDUCATION

The pseudo-intellectual element which will receive attention here conforms generally to a definite type. It consists in part of persons who have failed to complete training for the doctorate or, if they have earned such a degree, have done so at an inferior institution, thereby failing to attain the training which the academic doctorate implies. A common and characteristic trait of such people is a complete confidence in their own judgments on academic matters, however erroneous they may be, and extreme volubility in expressing these judgments.

A special group which exists within this classification is the often-called "rolling stones." They are unable to hold a teaching position for any great length of time in any institution, usually for no more than a single academic year, and move from one place to another as positions are open to them at their low salaries. As I have visited college after college over a period of years, I have met with these people in different settings. I recall having met one such person in an institution under examination by a committee of the Middle States Association of Colleges and Secondary Schools, of which I was chairman, and whom I recalled having met in another Catholic institution of higher education for women the year before. She came running up to me and pleaded: "Dr. Deferrari, don't let any member of your committee visit my classes in Spanish, because I don't know any Spanish!"

But these people are probably more to be pitied than blamed. With a false sense of economy some administrators of Catholic colleges, usually those conducted by nuns, employ such persons because they do not demand high salaries and are quite content to accept a teaching position which will give them a home and ordinary expense and spending money. I recall well one institution well known to Catholics, that paid these unfortunates $500.00 a year and gave them room and board. Of course, such teachers will not feel any great responsibility to keep their teaching on a very high level, even if they were able to do so, or to perform efficiently the minor technical duties that go with college teaching. Furthermore, they are frequently extremely critical of the administration and sometimes disrupt the morale of the other members of the faculty.

Another kind of teaching service that belongs in this category is a kind of exchange service. A religious community of men will agree to furnish such teachers as are required by a group of nuns in return for certain domestic help needed by the men or for any other comparable service. This is another bargain arrangement.

Sometimes members of the laity and of the secular clergy with most noble intentions will teach a course or two, over and above regular duties elsewhere, and refuse to take any salary in return. Rarely does such an arrangement result in a satisfactory college teaching situation. Again there is no control over the teacher.

I do not wish to give the impression that this failing is common in Catholic institutions of higher education. In fact, I believe that there is less of it now than there was twenty years ago. But in these days of the rise of many small colleges for women, and the constantly increasing cost of conducting colleges, especially for religious, a warning needs to be given and a positive method of defense against it needs to be stated.

Such members of the faculty as have just been described are very difficult to control by any administration. They realize that they are not being properly rewarded for the services which they render, and soon allow themselves to cut corners on rendering the duties expected of them. They will appear late for their classes or cut them frequently entirely. They will neglect the details of administration such as recording absences and tardiness and turning in grades promptly. The dean is at a complete loss as to how to deal with them.

The following procedures are urged:

(1) First of all a regular and worthy scale of salaries should be set up and all teachers should be paid accordingly. No exceptions should be made. If a faculty member should wish to donate his salary, he, of course, may do so.

(2) If board and room are included in the compensation, a definite equivalence in dollars and cents should be established.

(3) No one regardless of the terms involved should be permitted to teach who has not met at least the minimum requirements in the way of training for his teaching assignment.

(4) In the case specifically of the members of the laity, it is important for an administrator to learn the policies of the Association of American University Professors with reference to hiring and firing

teachers. These policies should be adhered to strictly. This will protect an institution against undesirable publicity when it becomes necessary to dismiss a member of the teaching staff.

(5) All regularly appointed teachers, if grades of appointment are used, from the rank of instructor through that of professor, are in the technical sense full members of the faculty. Regular meetings of the faculty should be held, at least twice a semester, and all members without exception should be invited to attend and take part in the appropriate business of the faculty.

By following these suggestions many faculty problems can be avoided.

CHAPTER ELEVEN

MEMBERS OF THE CLERGY AND LAITY AS
TEACHERS AND ADMINISTRATORS IN
CATHOLIC HIGHER EDUCATION

When I treated the topic in my *Memoirs*, [1] I
seemed to have over-simplified the problems involved. It might be said that I was still very much under
the influence of the ideas and policies of the earlier
rectors of the University, although in foot-note 2 of
page 342, by reason of later experience, I indicated
a definite weakening in my position as described in
the body of the chapter. This weakening on my part
was caused by my hearing two rectors say essentially
the following: "The members of the hierarchy are
very reluctant to give priests to the work of the Uni-

[1] Pages 340-342

137

versity and we need priests to run the University."
Of course this is true but we need laymen also. As
Cardinal Suenens [2] puts it: "The idea of the priest
as a complete entity in himself has been developed
too far: too has it been said that having recourse to
lay assistance was due to shortage of priests and
not, as it should be, part of the very nature of things.

"The idea of a priesthood cut off and isolated
from the laity is theological nonsense even before it
is a handicap to any effective apostolate. A priest
must be attached to the laity or his apostolate is par-
alyzed. His ministry loses, even before it starts, all
missionary character, for one obviously cannot be a
missionary in a vacuum.

"A priest whose function is not extended by the
cooperation of the laity is an anomaly, a contradiction.

"Lack of cooperation not only brings a real
danger of the priest being isolated and tempted to
despair in the face of the size of his task, it also
threatens to paralyze the laity by preventing them
from giving of their best."

So it is in an academic institution of higher education, members of the laity are just as indispensable
as the members of the clergy. They should be
welded together as a unit each performing his appropriate duty, with proper deference for the latter

[2] The Nun in the World, Westminster, Maryland, 1963,
pp. 98-99.

when required in the nature of things. The various functions to be performed in academic institutions will differ according to the character of each institution but they may all be arranged in the following three general classifications: (1) strictly for members of the clergy, such as chaplaincies and, in general, positions on faculties and in the administration of the schools of the sacred sciences, (2) especially for members of the laity, such as certain public relation activities and duties in the field of physical education, and (3) some, which in my *Memoirs* I have called indifferent, i. e. for members of either group according to their individual qualifications for the job. Those in this last classification are by far the more numerous. All this, of course, presumes that any activity which directly concerns faith and morals should be in the hands of the properly trained priest. Moreover, if the members of the clergy are to be sources of the rectors or presidents and other high officials in Catholic colleges and universities, then their academic training should include much more than the usual training of the theological seminary and even additional professional training.

The problem, however, has its solution in a more basic academic principle, in fact with a principle which, if applied strictly, will do no real violence to the ideas expressed above. All persons, whether cleric or laic should be appointed to a position only if he has the natural and acquired qualifications for that particular job. The practice of appointing a priest to an academic position simply because he has been ordained with little serious consideration of his qualifications to fill the needs of the post, is entirely too common in Catholic educational circles. This holds for religious communities of women, as well as for those of men, which conduct colleges and appoint their own members to key positions on the basis of seniority or for equally fatuous reasons. Unfortunately, this practice prevails too much all the way from the appointment of the proctor of a dormitory to that of a rector or president of a university. Many embarrassing and seriously harmful situations arise from this folly. Boards of trustees and other groups responsible for making academic appointments should examine carefully the professional qualifications involved and, if necessary, arrange for the appropriate training of the candidate either formally by his attending academic courses or informally by his association with successful occupants of like positions.

A word of warning needs to be expressed here. I have known religious communities to send someone destined to become dean or president of a college to a university to obtain a degree in higher education. The training which will thus be received will be not much better for the purpose than nothing, because it is the practical procedures which will be needed, and these will be received better and more efficiently from direct contact with those who have had the important experiences. Futhermore, the value of good academic training in content subjects, such as a doctorate in English or the Classics, is not to be underestimated for this purpose. A genuine sense of humility and a strong feeling of charity for one's fellow-man are strongly desired qualities in appointees to high academic places. I will not regale the reader with examples of the sad results of careless appointments of this kind. Some of them have been recorded in my Memoirs. Yet I might add that the mere fact that the holder of an important academic position has a right to do something (as a matter of fact, the more important the position, the stronger is his right to do whatever he pleases), does not justify his action nor enhance the good name and quality of his institution when he makes an egregious blunder of ignorance and lack of good judgment.

At this point I am urged to quote from the pastoral letter of Richard Cardinal Cushing, published on Good Shepherd Sunday, April, 1963. While His Eminence speaks specifically of the importance for a priest to keep up to date in his knowledge of the field of theology, his remarks apply equally as well to the necessity of his being and keeping well informed in whatever sphere the Lord may direct his activity.

"Within the Church our first concern should be directed toward a well-informed clergy. Providence has been kind to us in this respect and the training of priests in the United States generally has been of a high calibre. While for the gifted student the seminary may be less challenging than the university, the seminary function is a different one and requires an adaptation of university methods. Here is where the love of learning in the sacred sciences begins and is fostered. Here the mind is turned toward the pursuit of truth. But what of the years after ordination? The great advances in sacred knowledge each year offer new challenges to the priest, and resources must be provided on a continuing basis for 'refresher' opportunities for the clergy. We have experimented in a manner which has proven helpful, but it is plain that a greater effort is going to be required in the future. Here, of course, the apostolic endeavor of the priest himself must be the effective agent of action; he must never be satisfied with his present ecclesiastical learning but always eager to discover new spiritual and theological insights. Unless a priest's reading includes a body of recent writings in the sacred sciences he cannot expect to be an effective apostle to the people of his own generation. Clergy seminars must be more widely used with competent laymen invited to contribute in their field of specialization. The clergy will always set the measure of success for an informed public opinion because so many of the faithful will look to them, and rightly, for guidance and encouragement. . . .

"In his dealings with men, we recall that God ordinarly attains his ends through human agents using natural means. In our cooperation with this economy, the greatest natural means we can dedicate to God's service are those faculties which are specifically human: the intellect and the will. Cardinal Bea, in one of his recent lectures at Harvard University, stressed the part to be played by scholarship in the recovery of Christian unity, pointing out that the understanding of the past is the key to the present and that such understanding must be the preamble to reconciliation. Within the body of the Church, understanding is equally necessary to a fitting exchange of thought and opinion: understanding of the Church's nature, constitution and purpose; of her liturgy and spiritual life; of her history and of the world in which that history was lived. It is against this background of knowledge and understanding that public opinion has its immediate pertinence and lasting value."

Those properly concerned with the health and expansion of the Church are naturally uneasy sometimes about placing sensitive and important responsibilities in the hands of the members of the laity, over whom they appear to have little control. It seems to me that this problem takes care of itself in the natural course of events. The record of the life and activities of the lay person should be a sufficient guarantee against embarrassing or unwarranted action on his part.

As already intimated, a group of persons, composed of both members of the clergy and of the laity, all reasonably suited both by nature and by training as well as by experience for the duties which they are to perform, working together harmoniously for the development of an academic institution, is the great desideratum. In fact, most accrediting groups regularly seek the answer to the following question: "To what extent is there harmonious cooperation between all groups and individuals concerned with the welfare of the institution?"

Naturally, segregated faculty meetings, with the members of the laity excluded or included only when quite innocuous matters are discussed, the appointment of committees, in the more important of which the members of the laity are conspicuous by their absence, and similar examples of the exclusion of lay people simply because they are members of the laity, do not contribute to the harmony in a Catholic institution of higher education or to its effective administration.

CHAPTER TWELVE

CATHOLIC EDUCATORS AND THEIR RELATIONS WITH NON-CATHOLIC EDUCATORS

All educators, Catholic or non-Catholic, naturally have many common problems, by the discussion and investigation of which great profit may be gained by all. We are concerned here with the field of higher education only. This becomes increasingly true as the geographical circumference involved becomes smaller. Thus on a national, regional, and local scale this statement becomes more and more valid. The effect of a common attack on these problems is naturally greater and more successful.

Furthermore, Catholic educators cannot very well isolate themselves with impunity even if they should wish to do so. Any college or university

145

which has achieved any noteworthy success in its work will almost automatically create a reaction, good or bad, by whatever may happen within its confines, especially if it touches upon one of these common problems. Thus, if the authorities of an institution see fit to take action regarding freedom of speech and teaching which is directly contrary to the generally accepted policy of the educational world, or to its own proclaimed policy in this regard, the effect will be like the shot heard around the world. The news will travel fast and opinions respecting the good name of the college or university will be expressed in profusion. When an incident of this nature took place in one of the leading Catholic universities of the East, I personally received letters of inquiry from some leading non-Catholic educators asking if the horrible news could possibly be true.

Some situations arise when common action by educators and their institutions are badly needed. Thus in an emergency of war the need of fast spreading education is almost indispensable. The importance of a combined effort on the part of college personnel can be explained best by educators themselves. There are almost an endless number of peace time emergencies which call for an intelligent approach to a solution most effectively by the combined forces of educational groups.

Even more important and in need of all possible help and attention are certain educational problems themselves. As we have said many times before, educational opinion in the United States is formed by the educators themselves, and so educators are responsible for the formation and evolution of sound educational policies in the United States. We might even say that the general public has much to say in these matters, since the leading educators of the land are eager to present their ideas on educational problems to the people through articles and even books, and other popular media, since the people by their votes and through their representatives can influence greatly broad matters of educational policy. Thus the all important problem of national and central control of all education on a national scale has been held in check by a well formed public opinion on both a professional and popular level.

Another problem which becomes ever more difficult with the years is that of financing education in general, especially education under private auspices. [1] Private education on all levels must have financial support from individuals of wealth, established endowments, and the federal or state governments. Only a very few institutions have any great financial support from wealthy individuals

[1] Cf. Chapter entitled "Financing the Education of Students in Private Educational Institutions.

or foundations. The vast majority must look to the state and the federal governments. Most educators, even in public education, feel the tremendous importance of maintaining our private education. Only a very few, who by their very arguments show the narrowness of their points of view and their lack of any real knowledge of the history of world civilization, are vigorously opposed to assisting non-public education. We are convinced that a meeting of all interested parties on this problem would bring about a satisfactory solution.

There has always been a fear on the part of some Catholic educators that association of Catholic with non-Catholic educators will lead to some sort of contamination of ideas, and they would urge the policy of a "ghetto" for Catholic educators, in order to guarantee the purity of their educational philosophy. Such action seems to me like the height of folly. In any case, it seems to me to be worth the risk in order to leave the thinking of public educators with at least some of the ideas on education which we hold so fundamental. Furthermore, that influencing the thinking of public educators is not a fatuous thing, may be gathered from the fact that whenever an educational problem is before the government groups for consideration the educators called before them for consultation are always the representatives of non-Catholic groups and only rarely are Catholic educators summoned before them. In order to make the Catholic philosophy of education a real force in forming educational policy in the United States we must make ourselves felt in the thinking of these large non-sectarian educational groups.

It must be said, however, that Catholic educators, while cooperating and mingling with their non-Catholic brethren in facing the educational problems of the land, have the obligation of preserving the integrity of the basic principles of Catholic education. If these are clearly understood, as we have every reason to assume in this case, this should present no insurmountable difficulty.

CHAPTER THIRTEEN

CATHOLIC INSTITUTIONS OF HIGHER
EDUCATION AND PUBLIC OPINION [1]

Cardinal Cushing in his Pastoral Letter, The Church and Public Opinion, says (p. 4 f.): "In our national history, the Church for a long period experienced an atmosphere less than friendly and its immigrant members especially were subject to disabilities and even violence by reason of their faith. This often discouraged Catholics from taking a part in civil affairs. Instead of being able to participate in the formation of the public opinion on which the life of a democracy so largely depends, they found

---

[1] Cf. "The Church and Public Opinion," a Pastoral Letter by Richard Cardinal Cushing, Archbishop of Boston. Boston: Daughters of St. Paul, 1963

public opinion set in advance against them. This forced on them a reactive isolation. It encouraged a minority attitude that, while dismissing accomplishments of others, prided itself on the actions of Catholics that merited public notice. This mentality is even now occasionally manifest, but it is a relic of an earlier and less happy time.

"Catholics have also held aloof from some activities because of the need they have felt to safeguard standards upheld uniquely by the Church. In several important areas, however—one thinks of politics and labor—their policy has been that which was expressed by Cardinal Gibbons when he rejected the idea that Catholics should form separate labor unions, such as those in Europe, lest the faithful be contaminated by mixing with anarchists and socialists. He pointed out in that context that this was 'one of the trials of faith which our brave American Catholics are accustomed to meet almost daily and which they know how to disregard with good sense and firmness.'

"The intensification of antireligious thought, successive waves of Catholic immigrants and increased discrimination against Catholics continued to place the Church in a merely protective position, and, in some measure, hindered Catholic participation in the affairs of the nation.

"The impetus toward free expression by the laity as members of the Church and as American citizens was not entirely lost but it was so greatly diminished that when the tide turned again in the other direction in these last years it seemed to some like a new beginning. Since the 1920's, however, there has been evident a growing participation of the laity in the activities of the Church and a growing influence of Catholics on the life of the country. This has come about partly because of the growth in the Catholic population and its increased material resources and education. The formative impetus, however, has come from the movements which make up the renewal that is going on in the Church in our days: the revival of the doctrine of the Mystical Body, the liturgical movement, the emphasis on the role of the laity in the social apostolate, and *the development of a theology of the spiritual life of the laity. This last, especially, with the growing attention to spiritual formation and studies in theology, has set the revival of lay participation on the firmest of foundations.*"[1]

While the Cardinal is speaking of public opinion in general, his discussion, of which necessarily only a small portion has been quoted, applies very forcefully to Catholic higher education in particular. The entire matter of public opinion is tied up with the place of the layman in the work of the Church. I do not wish to enter upon this important and somewhat complex subject with any detail.

[1] The italics are mine.

Rather will I dismiss it with another quotation from the Cardinal's pastoral letter (pp. 20 f.), and confine myself to a discussion of the general topic of public opinion as it relates to Catholic institutions of higher education.

"Since the lay person in the Church brings with him his own abilities and talents, these in a particular way should find constructive expression, The *scientist, the scholar, the teacher,*[1] *the doctor, the lawyer, the public servant,* and all the rest, have something to say which can make the Church a more effective instrument of grace for the good of souls. When these voices are silent the Church suffers from their loss and the Christian has abdicated his responsibility toward the Kingdom. We must acknowledge regretfully that many of our people have traditionally maintained an almost passive attitude in this regard, thinking it sufficient for them to be faithful to Mass and the Sacraments and certain acts of personal devotion."

In the Introduction to this work, I referred briefly to the accreditation of educational institutions in the United States, and to the fact that above the level of the department of education of the individual states the approval and supervision of education in the United States was in the hands of the institutions themselves, which had organized into various associations for this purpose. Catholic

[1] The italics are mine.

educators and persons of importance in the direction and administration of the works of the Church until comparatively recently were bitterly opposed to representatives of Catholic educational institutions having anything whatever to do with these groups. I recall very vividly when I first came to the University, being quite unaware of the educational attitudes of the people among whom I was to live for the next fifty years of my life, referring very frankly to the educational contacts which I presumed the University was having with these non-Catholic educators. This took place at a faculty meeting of the now defunct School of Letters. I received a very vigorous reproof for daring even to think of any fraternizing with such educators. That this was not an isolated case, I lived to see a few years later in a similar experience suffered by a new and well-meaning colleague. This attitude was very widespread and intense approximately fifty years ago. Some Catholic educators venture to say today in a rather uncomplimentary way that The Catholic University of America enjoys wide membership in and greater respect educationally from these groups because the spirit of aloofness from them was not so intense within it as within other Catholic institutions of higher education. In any case, it may be said that in those early days Catholic education was confined rather strictly of its own volition to an educational ghetto.

Attitudes have changed greatly, however, over recent years. I can remember vividly being the only representative of a Catholic educational institution at very important local and national meetings. I recall also hearing the president of a large Catholic university in a meeting of the regional association object strenuously that Deferrari was the only representative of a Catholic institution holding any position of importance in the group, as if this situation were due to ill-will on anyone's part rather than to the failure of himself and his colleagues to appreciate the value of good public opinion in the field of education. But there has been a great change, fortunately, in recent years. The meetings of these same educational groups are crowded to capacity with sisters, priests, and at least some members of the laity. The chief complaint lies in the fact that the sisters express themselves on important issues very rarely, and laymen hardly more so. There appears to be among the latter a feeling that they would be out of place speaking in behalf of or in respect to any phase of Catholic education. This is definitely unfortunate, and it is to be hoped that this too will pass away.

Periodically, a Catholic educator, usually a priest, will rise at a meeting of Catholic educators and speak indignantly for the formation of a scheme of accreditation for Catholic instiutions only and the abandonment of our relationship with the existing national groups. This, of course, would be a return to the ghetto existence, and I would refer such as these to Cardinal Gibbons' feelings about separate labor unions. Of course, Catholics should not have a separate accrediting plan, [1] but there is every reason why Catholic educators should take an active part in the work of the existing educational groups and make themselves felt in them.

A situation exists today in the general field of education which arose from our ghetto days. Probably the two largest and most influential groups in existence today are the National Education Association and the National Catholic Educational Association. Neither of these is an accrediting association, but both have a tremendous influence in the field of American education. While an increasing number of Catholics are joining the N.E.A., the group is extremely small and essentially of no influence in forming the policies of the Association. Indeed, the policies and philosophy of this group are in most instances diametrically opposed to those acceptable to Catholic educators. The unfortunate result of this is that when representatives of this group are consulted, they are to be assumed to be giving the opinions of American educators as a whole. Furthermore, there is a distinct feeling of hostility between the members of both groups for each other.

[1] Cf. Memoirs, pp. 280 and 281.

When I took part in the United States Education Mission to Japan, [1] directly after World War II, it was clearly evident from the membership that it was strongly dominated by the N.E.A., in spite of the fact that Monsignor Hochwalt and myself were supposed to represent the Catholic point of view. In the last days of the Mission, when the final report was being drawn up, Monsignor Hochwalt was obliged to leave for the United States and I found myself alone to represent the philosophy of Catholic education.[2] I cannot say that Catholic education fared badly in this report. Certainly, the Apostolic Delegate, Archbishop Paul Morella, was well satisfied with the result. But this was accomplished in no way by the support of the N.E.A. Not infrequently there were clashes between the two ideologies and usually from lack of numbers we were forced to give way and remain silent.

My feeling is that from the beginning we should have taken our place in the N.E.A. and helped mold its policies, and so make it a true representative body of American educators. Perhaps it is not too late to make it such in the future, but there is a strong feeling of antipathy and aloofness on both sides. I make bold to state that if the N.C.E.A. had never been formed but the N.E.A. had taken in all the Catholic educators now secluded

[1] Cf. Memoirs, pp. 381-396.
[2] Cf. Memoirs, pp. 395-396.

in the confines of the N.C.E.A., Catholic education working within the N.E.A. and establishing a high level of public opinion would be much more influential today. I wish to state at this point that I am making no reference whatsoever here to the National Catholic Welfare Conference.

There has always been a feeling among Catholics themselves that publications by our people ordinarily do not reach the wide American public.[1] This, all in all, we believe to be true. The causes are varied and have already been mentioned. Part of the explanation, however as Cardinal Cushing[2] says, "must lie in our own unwillingness, our own lack of confidence, or our own neglect. Laity and clergy alike have failed here, and a common burden rests upon us all to correct the situation."

Before closing this chapter I would like to refer to another statement of Cardinal Cushing[3] regarding the layman's place in this matter: "Once again, we must emphasize that the lay person in the Church has the greater opportunity for bearing witness to the vitality of the Church in the world than the clergy, or even the higher Church authorities. In his professional and personal life he is judged by friends and acquaintances, as if he were the entire

---

[1] See also Chapter Five on "The Problems of Research in Catholic Institutions of Higher Education."

[2] *Op. cit.* p. 30.

[3] My experiences include several unpleasant incidents caused through feelings of bigotry by this very confusion.

Church, not one member of it. In point of fact, he creates public opinion, unconsciously, maybe even unwillingly, making up men's minds about the Church by his every word and action."

In my own experience, as I attended a great many meetings within the field of higher education, I can bear witness to the truth of these words. I can recall several occasions when sitting at the conference table with my non-Catholic friends, having one of them look at me intently and saying: "Deferrari, do you have orders?" I was a little shocked as well as puzzled at first, but, when I recovered and asked several questions in return, I discovered that in spite of my collar and tie they thought that I was an ordained priest. Furthermore, on almost every occasion I was treated with a courtesy and kindness that would do honor to any duly ordained clergyman.

CHAPTER FOURTEEN

PROBLEMS IN HIGHER EDUCATION
FOR SISTERS

The education of Sisters had reached a stubborn impass after the turn of the century when opportunities for higher education were practically closed to them by reason of their close adherence to the old world ideas of the religious life. Then the Very Reverend Thomas Edward Shields broke the stalemate by his startling conception of an institution of higher education for Sisters only, the Sisters College of The Catholic University of America. Dr. Shields' careful organization and adminstration of this institution made the idea acceptable to Catholic educators generally, and similar institutions sprang up throughout the land.

Through the next half century or a little more the higher education of Sisters found itself slipping into another block, as it were, largely through the pressure of outside forces. The great increase in the American population produced crowded schools and more numerous institutions than the religious teachers could care for. Very harmful to the growth of the religious life was the fact that superiors, in order to meet the excessive demand for teaching Sisters, sent them out into the classroom before their religious and intellectual formation was completed. The shortage of Sisters, moreover, was aggravated by the demand for religious in the professions—nursing and social work especially. The vain attempt to meet the ever increasing demand for religious workers by cutting down on their training was bound to have a very deleterious effect. The solution of the problem seemed impossible.

Then at a meeting of the National Catholic Educational Association in 1957, held at St. Louis, Sister M. Emil, I.H.M., startled her audience by a frank general presentation of the shortcomings of the training of Sisters both for the religious life as well as for their teaching duties. From this beginning has arisen what is widely known today as the Sister Formation Conference. Its influence has been tremendous and is difficult to gauge. It will continue to be great under proper direction, but much remains to be done. It is unreasonable to expect that it has done more than make a beginning. The greatest accomplishment is the fact that it has broken what might be called the lock-step of the education of nuns. There is now almost a universal awareness of a need for a more efficient training for nuns, a general background training which will serve both for the religious and the professional life as a unit.

Some of the problems which face the nuns in this all important matter are contained in the following quotation from a "policy-resolution" adopted at the August, 1962, Leadership Meeting.

"The Conference does not consider small numbers nor an all-Sister student body a cause or sign of weakness in a college. It respects the autonomy of each congregation and the legitimate desire of a religious group to educate its members under optimum conditions for the preservation and enhancement of its religious spirit. It recognizes, finally, that new institutions must begin before they can grow or achieve recognition.

"The Conference feels, moreover, that injudiciously publicized criticisms of Sisters' Colleges, often set up because of conditions under which religious groups have little or no control, do no good and may work real harm.

"On the other hand, the Conference wishes to record that it has never advocated the establishment of colleges which could not achieve regional accreditation within a reasonable time. It deplores the erection of such colleges as a hazard to the good name of all Catholic colleges and universities and to the general effectiveness of Catholic education."

Then this document proceeds to urge these small colleges to use the consultative services of the regional accrediting agencies and to seek full accreditation as soon as possible after their foundation.

This document, all in all, is excellent. My only criticisms of it pertain to emphasis and are minor. Thus, I would say that the emphasis on the regional accreditating associations is ill-conceived. These groups have done and are doing Catholic education a great deal of good, but they do make mistakes and should by no means be followed almost blindly. For example, their stand on so-called academic inbreeding leaves much to be desired. [1]

My own strong feeling is that every college, Catholic or otherwise, should be evaluated on the basis of its own intrinsic merits. The faculty should be judged on the quality of its training and achievement. If there is any great indication of the sameness and routine, which is usually associated with academic inbreeding, the institution should be criticized and penalized accordingly. To be critical of a faculty merely because its members as a whole or in any great number have their first degrees from the same institution seems to me to be a reversion to the super-

[1] See Handbook for Catholic Higher Education, Chapter 14b.

ficial and mechanical evaluative criteria which most of us had hoped were things of the past! Furthermore, individuals connected in some way with these groups often speak with authority which they do not possess and must be given heed with great circumspection. Then also, I do not believe that a college for nuns approved by its Department of State to grant degrees and possessing the accreditation of its own State Department of Education but not approved by its regional association will do Catholic education any real harm. Actually, it can well do much good for its own religious group and for Catholic education in general.

All the problems which the nuns face in the higher education of the members of their own communities are not contained in the document just discussed. It may be said that all persons who plan to enter a religious community of women should be expected to have the necessary qualities to procure and profit by a general education. The extent to which they can and will so profit will depend on the individual and the guidance which she will receive in the matter. The Sister Formation Conference, to its high credit, has from the start preached this principle. This does not mean, of course, that those who are convinced that they have a religious vocation but cannot for the lack of a sufficiently strong intellectual endowment follow through with the regular program of studies are to be rejected. Adjustments both in training and in future duties have to be made. But after the training for the first degree a tremendous responsibility rests upon religious superiors if the community and the Church are to realize the full potentiality of our young womanhood. It seems to me that there has been and is a great waste of badly-needed talent here.

The problem of deciding who shall go on for higher studies, in what subjects, and where is a most difficult one. Some persons have the intellectual acumen to continue with their studies but have a strong aversion to any great intellectual activity. Regardless of what we may think of their intellectual laziness, it is a mistake to request that such persons be asked to do so. They will not concentrate as they should on these higher studies and the result will be someone who is neither a good teacher nor a worthy scholar. Obviously before a decision is reached in any case, the Sister should be consulted very tactfully and sympathetically. It should be mentioned here that many a young Sister with a genuine potentiality for higher studies has been lost to the Community and the Church by a hasty decision to place her in some routine post, even in teaching, for which many Sisters in the Community are not only available but eager to enter.

Assuming then that the Sister is at least not completely averse to higher study, the question arises as to what field of work she should be asked to enter.

The needs of the Community deserve some consideration but they should by no means be the compelling factor. As a former dean of a graduate school I can say with confidence that the student's natural interests, granting a proper preliminary training, usually forecasts his future success in the higher studies of his choosing.

The next step is to select a graduate school which has an outstanding department in the field into which the student wishes to enter. It seems almost too obvious to mention that all graduate schools are not strong in all departments. Inquiry of well known scholars in the field will help greatly in making the final decision. Also, the determining factor in arriving at the selection is the fact that the Community has an institution of some kind in the vicinity of a graduate school, at which the student may room and board. This unfortunately is often the weight that turns the scales in favor of an inferior department of study. Of course, the additional cost of paying for board and room where the Sister can go for high quality supervision and direction in her gradate studies is not to be compared with the training and formation which the Sister will bring home to the motherhouse. Not infrequently, when a Sister has finally become settled in a worthy department with an outstanding scholar to direct her work, a superior will attempt to settle the details of her program, about which she knows little or nothing. Again

I speak from very unpleasant experience. The community needs someone not only to teach history in the college but some elementary chemistry. Why cannot the Sister visit the institution's course in that subject, and take down the notes to bring back home for regurgitation at her own college is a typical question. All this would be ludicrous, were it not true and not of infrequent occurrence. Once the graduate student has been selected and all the details of work as described above have been settled, the Sister should be left alone in the hands of those responsible for her higher education.

Another problem involved in the training of Sisters to assume a position of intellectual and scholarly importance is the development of an appropriate general maturity, especially in her field of specialization. This is realized best by having theoretical and personal contact with the members of the laity and those outside the Church. Moreover, it can be had very appropriately at meetings of the learned societies, both Catholic and non-sectarian in the field. The naiveté and general uncertainty with which some Sisters speak at these mixed meetings is most embarrassing, to put it mildly.

In this connection, it should be added that the common belief among religious communities of women that once a person has obtained a doctorate in a field she has enough training and information to last her for the rest of her life is a most unwarranted assumption. The final problem for a superior, after the formal training of her nuns for teaching in an institution of higher education has been ended, is to encourage them to keep up to date in their fields by doing worthwhile research themselves and by attending and taking part in the proceedings of learned societies. These Sisters need encouragement as well as appreciation from higher authority. But they also need time and should not be saddled with a multiplicity of duties and then learn that they have been listening to mere lip-service from their superiors on the value of research. If they do not have time in their regular schedule, the only recourse a serious minded Sister has for the continuation of the research which she has learned to value is to use her leisure. Thus she loses the benefit of much needed recreation. There are, of course, many practical household tasks that must be attended to in a college conducted by a religious community, but services cannot be divided three and four ways by one person. Teaching and research are distinct from counseling and proctoring, and often the requirements of the two interfere with each other. There needs to be a clear division of duties among persons. Again, if they had their training in an outstanding graduate department, there will be no danger of the development of pride. In fact, by the very nature of things humility will unconsciously and naturally impress itself upon them every step of the way.

CHAPTER FIFTEEN

THE RELIGIOUS COMMUNITY COLLEGE
FOR WOMEN

Many believe that the college conducted chiefly, if not exclusively, for the members of a religious community is a new kind of institution of higher education which came into existence under the stimulus of the Sister Formation Conference. It is true that such institutions arose in great numbers under the encouragement of this Conference and for the first time then came to the attention of educators in general.

Small religious communities have always faced the difficulty of giving their postulants and novices an adequate training both for the religious life and for the professional activities, including teaching, which they were destined to enter. Unfortunately in the past, especially, this training, except possibly

169

on the religious side, was not faced squarely. An erroneous kind of confidence was placed in the Holy Spirit to carry these young women through their initial difficulties in the professions. Eventually through hard experience they found the solution to many of their problems. Some of their difficulties, however, naturally remained unsolved even to the end.

At the present time probably the greatest weakness in the training of religious women lies in preparing them for their work in the foreign missions. A special program, over and above the usual training, is needed. A speaking knowledge of the native language in question is fundamental, we are told by experienced workers in the field, and some knowledge of the culture and civilization should be acquired, if the natives are to receive them with confidence and even friendliness. Most of the religious groups, including the larger ones, fail in this. Perhaps it is too much to expect the religious community itself to furnish this instruction. In such cases, the prospective foreign missioner should be sent to a Catholic college or university where a training to meet the need can be obtained. Such institutions do exist, but I fear that our Catholic institutions of higher education have not done enough along these lines to meet the problem fully.

The basic reason, however, for the existence of the college of the religious community of women is of course to train women to be good members of the particular religious community. This main and all important purpose has in the past been interfered with by a number of pressures for the services of the nuns. The strongest and probably the most damaging interference has been the demand for elementary school teachers. This resulted in programs of study of a normal school character rather than of a general nature in keeping with the formation of women for the religious life. Thanks to the wisdom of the Sister Formation Conferene, the pressure has been eliminated somewhat. There is certainly much universal agreement that these colleges should have a general program of liberal arts, and this certainly is to be commended.

Some of the features of these colleges vary among themselves according to the educational theories of the religious communities concerned. Thus certain ones insist that to achieve the purposes which they have set up for themselves, so called "outsiders," i.e. non-members of the religious community, should not be received as students; others declare that the association of non-religious with the religious in the period of college training is beneficial for all concerned. Indeed, this policy has brought the opportunities for college training to the young ladies of many remote areas. Some look upon the religious community college as a stepping stone to a regular four year institution open to the general public. At this point those aiming for final profession of religious vows are given special courses by themselves for this purpose. The successful development of colleges such as these has resulted in a rather large number of such institutions, and the movement should be encouraged and assisted in every way possible.

The chief problems involved affect small religious communities, and their efforts to establish institutions of their own have sometimes been severely criticized, even by Catholic educators. Some of these religious communities are small by the very reason of their basic organizational principles. When they reach a certain size a group splits off and sets up a new motherhouse in some region where a need for their services is apparent. Thus, they remain small, but the need of training centers for their subjects always remains with them. Such groups may take comfort in the educational criterion that any college should be regarded as a good institution, provided that it sets its goal within a range that it can reach successfully. There are colleges and institutions large of enrollment but by reasons of methods of instruction and faulty organization fall far short of their goals.

The following remarks were made with more or less justification perhaps by the Commission on Institutions of Higher Education of the Middle States Association of Colleges and Secondary Schools: [1]

[1] Document No. 4. 37.

"The limited enrollment such colleges some-times have is not in itself a barrier to Middle States membership, but a very small student body creates certain problems for any institution. A primary one, especially in a religious community, is that of main-taining a numerous and varied enough faculty to provoke continuous and many sided professional discussion among its members, present them contin-uously with new interests and points of view, and excite their scholarly activity; to generate, in short, an intellectual climate which favors the vigorous scholarship and stimulating teaching which ought to be among the high rewards of academic life.

"Another problem with a very small student body and faculty is to provide enough courses to give the curriculum proportion and adaptability to the individual. Another is to foster, when the stu-dents are few and homogeneous, the interaction and competition among them which is as important ed-ucationally as personal instruction is.

"As a result a religious community which wants its own college of high quality must be prepared for greater per-student costs than a larger institution would face. It is especially important that all the members of a small faculty should have superior training in a diversity of graduate schools in the sub-jects they teach."

This is sufficient to give the general tenor of the adverse criticisms of the small religious community for women. In themselves they are justified but sufficient or even no cognizance is taken of the fact that nearly all those responsible for these institutions have taken the trouble to get full information on the problem involved. As to the small numbers and the resultant disadvantages, the fact remains that small religious communities actually grow when good instruction is provided their new members. Furthermore, anyone acquainted with religious life knows that with well-trained teachers from the Community's members, the "many sided professional discussion" and "the new interests and points of view" continue within the community with the teachers themselves members of the community more effectively than when the students have to travel even short distances to an over-crowded class and hurry right back to the convent with scarcely receiving a nodding acquaintance with the teacher.

Many other answers might be given to the criticisms of this document. Of the many religious communities which I have visited in connection with the establishment of an educational institution, I have yet to find any superior who did not regard the establishment of a community college not only as a benefit to the members who were to attend its classes but to all the community, old members as well as those of recent profession. The building up of the library as a collection of books is a boon to everyone, not merely for the attending students, and the cost cheap at almost any price.

The Commission on Institutions of Higher Education of the Middle States Association of Colleges and Secondary Schools and similar groups are in my opinion well disposed towards the Religious Community College for Women, and are ready to help them in every way with which they are familiar. But many of the individual members of these groups have mistaken notions about the ability and knowledge of the religious superiors concerned. These erroneous ideas unfortunately have in some cases been fostered by Catholics themselves. All this usually comes to the surface when an evaluation group reports on the result of its visitation to a religious community college. The recommendations made in some cases are quite ridiculous and exhibit abysmal ignorance of the nature of the institution which they have evaluated. With sympathetic understanding the religious superiors will in nearly every instance carry out successfully the projects which they have undertaken.

Of course, the religious superiors must be ready first of all to appraise their educational needs and their resources to meet them. They must then push forward and stick steadfastly to their task. As a matter of fact it is a task which is essentially never completed but which must be pursued constantly.

CHAPTER SIXTEEN

THE CATHOLIC JUNIOR COLLEGE

A junior college has been defined as a college providing courses of freshman, and often sophomore grade, either as an independent unit or as a part of a standard college or of a secondary school. It received its greatest impetus as the general level of education in the United States gradually reached graduation from high school and opportunities for employment for several reasons became comparatively less and demanded better training.

No satisfactory definition of a junior college has as yet been forthcoming. Frankly, I see no great need of a specific one, just as long as we think of a two year post secondary school institution, which,

176

as F. Taylor Jones, Executive Secretary of the Middle States Commission on Institutions of Higher Education, has put it, has "clear and realistic concepts of (a) its functions, and (b) its educational objectives for its students." In other words, the junior college is a post secondary school institution which over a two year period is meeting certain educational needs of a community. I do not intend to go into a more detailed discussion of this problem. It seems to me that difficulties arise when an attempt is made to set up a rigid definition and to expect every professed junior college to follow it. Like all successful educational movements the junior college must be free.

The following information in outline depicts the beginning and the growth of the junior college movement in the United States. [1]

Beginnings of the junior college:

1835   First *private* junior college, Godfrey, Illinois.

1875   Junior colleges urged in address to National Educational Association by the President of the University of Minnesota.

1900   Junior colleges suggested by William Raney Harper, University of Chicago.

1901   First *public* junior college, Joliet, Illinois. This is still in operation.

---

[1] I am indebted to Sister Teresa Aloyse, President of Immaculata College, Washington, D.C., for this summary.

Growth of junior colleges:

1922   207 junior colleges, enrolling 16,031 (average 77 each)

1963   700 junior colleges, enrolling 800,000 (average over 1,000 each)

Earliest Catholic junior colleges:

1928   26 Catholic junior colleges
3 founded 1900 or earlier
4 founded 1900-1920
19 founded 1920-1927

1963   2 (of the 26) are still listed as junior colleges. All the others have
    a) become four-year colleges or universities or
    b) ceased to operate as institutions of higher education.

Present situation of Catholic junior colleges:

1963   The Directory of American Association of Junior Colleges lists:
700 junior colleges
220 under religious denominations
62 are Roman Catholic (one is Byzantine)
Most of them are juniorates or seminaries
20 Catholic junior colleges serve the public

The President's Commission on Higher Education in 1948 set up the principle that at least two years of education beyond high school should be made available to all persons able to profit by such an opportunity. As a result more than half the states and many local school districts have established programs for one, two, and three years beyond high school. These junior colleges are supported largely by taxation, local and state. It is worthy of note that federal legislation supporting higher education includes junior colleges.

This great upsurge in the establishment of junior colleges immediately raised the question in the minds of educators as to whether the junior college was to be regarded as secondary or higher education, and this uncertainty caused some confusion at the time. It was difficult to see how, if, as the Truman Committee urged, these two years of instruction after graduation from high school were to be attached to the various public school systems, the nature of the instruction could be other than that of the secondary school. Furthermore, the surroundings and the atmosphere of the entire educational unit would of necessity be those of the secondary school, and at least some of the faculty for obvious reasons, chiefly financial, would be drawn from the secondary school staff. This was an important matter which needed settlement, since this would affect the approval by the various accrediting agencies in the evaluation of junior colleges.

Educators in general now regard the junior colleges as higher education. The trend is entirely that way today, especially since all the regional accrediting so regard it, basing their accrediting procedure rather fully on the procedures for evaluating four year colleges.

It is difficult to determine definitely the identifying features of the junior college other than to say that the program of studies is usually of two academic years duration. In the beginning the custom was for both Catholic and non-Catholic two year institutions to regard themselves as essentially the the first two years of a senior or four year college. Even today, practically all the two or three year institutions of religious communities are of this nature. In other words, they have one program, a so-called transfer program, since their students are for the most part following a scheme of studies which will enable them to transfer to a four-year institution and obtain a bachelor's degree. But some educators have refused to recognize such institutions as *bona fide* junior colleges. Such students, they say, might well go to a senior college and attend for only two academic years with the same result. They insist, and rightly so, that a unified and well rounded program of two years of college work is far different and superior to the first two years lopped off a four year college program. Yet some four year colleges try to conduct a two year program simultaneously with the regular four year curriculum.

The chief outstanding characteristics of the junior college may be regarded as follows:

(1) Entrance requirements are lower. Frequently students are accepted in a junior college who would not be acceptable to the average general college. This does not mean, however, that entrance requirements are to be thrown to the winds. Some standards must be set up, although not necesarily of a quality considered better than average for a senior college. Most senior colleges, especially in these days of bulging enrollments, will give little consideration to secondary school students in the lowest fifth of their graduating class, but junior college administrators feel it to be their duty to examine them and discover some who under the special treatment of their institution will develop into good college material.

(2) The so-called transfer program may be carried on for the very laudable purpose of developing students who are seriously concerned about obtaining a degree from a senior college, so that they can meet the demands of the general college on graduation from the lesser institution, which they could not have done two years earlier. Several public junior colleges, Catholic and non-Catholic, have been very successful in this.

(3) But no two year institutions, leaving out those conducted by religious communities for their own members, are concerned primarily with the so-

called transfer program, but rather with the terminal programs. These may be of the most varied kinds including some of the trades and minor professions, for example, bed-side nursing, dentist's assistants, cosmotology, and others.

(4) Circumstances prevent some students from spending more than two years in college. This they know before they enter the freshman class. They naturally prefer to enter an institution that will give them a well rounded and complete program.

(5) Some junior colleges feel it within their province to offer a program which will train young women to take their place in a society of some high degree of culture. This might be stated in another way, to offer an asylum, as it were, for young women who are looking forward to an early marriage.

Some colleges, including several under Catholic auspices, feel justified in conducting two year or junior college programs simultaneously with their four year programs. In view of the characteristics of the junior college which have been presented above, it is difficult to understand how this can be done effectively. There is a temptation to do this in the belief that the enrollment and financial income will be greatly increased. Rather will such a policy drive potentially good students elsewhere and ultimately impair the growth of the institution. The college will definitely have the image of a junior college among the people from whom it hopes to draw its students. According to the standards of an acceptable senior college, inferior students will infiltrate with the good ones and impede their progress. The purposes of the two kinds of institutions will definitely clash and impede the achievement of the purpose of each. On the other hand, a large institution of complex organization, like a university, could have among its various schools and colleges, each more or less independent of all other segments, collegiate offerings organized as a junior college leading to junior college degrees and diplomas. This would require very careful planning and an abundance of funds. Unfortunately, this is not the way in which it is usually done. It is the small college that most often attempts to bring about the marriage of the two, and usually with disastrous results.

In any case, it cannot be said that the junior college has flourished on Catholic soil. It is very difficult to say how many public junior colleges there are today under Catholic auspices, because they change their junior college status and become four year colleges so rapidly. Significant statistics have been given earlier in this discussion. Very few Catholic junior colleges have started out with the aims and purposes of a junior college definitely in mind and with a determination to become an outstanding junior college and to remain so indefinitely. Several, however, have done so very successfully, and these are all for women. The Catholic junior college for men is practically non-existent.

A glance at the statistics given earlier in this discussion is enough to prove the widespread need and acceptance of the non-Catholic junior college. It would be interesting to learn how many of the students enrolled are Catholic. Certainly Catholics are not so different from the rest of the population that they feel no need of the junior college in their educational system. Then why are there so few of them under Catholic auspices? Some say: "Because Catholic educators do not understand them and the part which they play in higher education." The answer to me seems to be one of lack of finances and resources generally. Catholics are thinking seriously of curtailing the educational system which they have already developed without the junior college. The sources of financial assistance are comparatively meagre indeed. Religious vocations have not increased to the point where they are sufficient for existing educational institutions. Shall we add to our educational responsibilities by establishing a system of junior colleges? Certainly we need them to counteract the attraction of the numerous non-Catholic junior colleges. Perhaps the resources will soon be available by increased and more widespread government aid, and perhaps the number of religious vocations will grow larger in our changing world.

The following two predictions are startling and especially worthy of note. They should spur Catholic educators to give very serious thought to the place and importance of the junior college in the Catholic school system.

1. By 1970 half of all college students in the United States will be in junior colleges. This prediction was made at the Midwest Junior College Conference, Kansas City, July, 1963.

2. Everyone will pass from a junior college with an A.A. (Associate of Arts) or A.S. (Associate of Science) degree by the year 2,000. Universities will have dropped freshman and sophomore years. Graduates from junior college will enroll for a three-year program leading to a master's degree. [1] This, of course, in a general way is a reversion to the educational system of the leading countries of Europe. In fact it has been tried in this country at the University of Chicago.

[1] Cf. AMERICA, July, 1963, p. 45, quoting from the March 1963 issue of the Bulletin of the Association of American Colleges.

CHAPTER SEVENTEEN

STATE AND REGIONAL ACCREDITATION: BEFORE AND AFTER

The practical educational philosophy of some Catholic eduators, not many to be sure but entirely too many for the best interests of Catholic education, is sometimes very alarming. I refer to an inadequate understanding of the basic principles involved in the developement of truly Catholic institutions. This, moreover, results, perhaps for practical reasons, in an over-readiness to follow blindly the guidance of state departments of education and also that of regional associations, and in so doing to feel no need of Catholic direction and consciously or unconsciously to allow themselves to be cut off from its influences.

Thus there is always the danger that the Catholic educator will tend to be greatly over-awed by the power of the state department of education, I might even say, baffled by the educational demands which it lays down. This is even more true with their relations with the regional association. All effort and resources are directed toward meeting those requirements with little or no thought of the implications involved. In other words such educators lose their independence of mind in educational matters and permit others, who often are understandably unable to get to the root of the difficulties of Catholic institutions, to do their thinking for them. Furthermore, this is only a part of the difficulty. After they have assimilated the educational principles of these groups and have become very glib in quoting them and, finally, after they have achieved them and obtained the desired approval, they immediately become relieved of all anxiety about their educational problems and fall back into a state of complete desuetude in their educational thinking. The millenium has been reached! What more needs to be done! They have never done any systematic and constructive thinking about the future development of their institution. Their thoughts have been circumscribed by the demands at the moment of the state and the regional groups. Once these have been met, according to their thinking, nothing more remains to be accomplished, a most depressing and ruinous state of mind for any educator and a disastrous situation for the institution which he directs. In such an attitude of academic smugness, they may even go so far as to cut themselves off from any Catholic contact which they may have had. We are a good institution, they say; we have reached regional accreditation acquired through our own efforts; we can stand on our own feet; we need no one's help. They seem to have no realization of the fact that a close contact with educators who share their objectives, and who through wide and long experience are able to be helpful to them, is no sign of weakness but rather the mark of wisdom. As in all important activities humility in education is a precious asset.

There are many practical and demonstrable reasons, it seems to me, which compel Catholic educators to stand united and to pool their intellectual resources when facing their problems, even after they have met the demands of non-Catholic groups and despite the values which those demands may have in themselves. Catholic education needs assistance and guidance in many matters in which our own non-Catholic brethren have little or no competence. Some of these I propose to discuss briefly here. However, first of all, it should be made clear that in the opinion of many Catholic educators, all-in-all, educational officials of both the state and regional associations have over the years been very helpful to Catholic education. It is by no means an over-statement to say that Catholic education in the United States would never have accomplished what it has up to this time had it not been for the sympathy and devoted interest of these persons. In fact, some of them are themselves devout Catholics. But, by and large, their background training does not permit them to see and appreciate the important differences, even though they may appear slight at times, between a scheme of education which is centered around Catholic philosophy (in the strict sense) and theology and a system which must of necessity divest itself completely of these subjects. Proper educational contacts with these fields are not always easy. On the contrary, there is always a real danger of falling into a mechanical procedure and of unconsciously paying mere lip service to what philosophy and theology can and should contribute to Catholic education. Moreover, the details of the manner in which these two subjects can best make themselves felt, that is, be properly integrated with all courses of whatever level, have by no means been satisfactorily worked out. Much still remains to be done.

It should then be obvious to the Catholic educator that there is a need in our modern educational system for two kinds of assistance in continued development. There is no question in my mind that accreditating groups in general have played and will continue to play a most important part in the development of our Catholic educational institutions. I am equally certain, however, that there is a special need in their continuing development which can be filled only by Catholic professional educational groups. The future of American Catholic education lies in the cooperative assistance of both, based on a recognition on the part of Catholic educators that general educational excellence can in no way be equated with accreditation of any kind, state or regional.

Lest these generalities be questioned for lack of precision, it may be well to point out certain important areas within which Catholic higher education, and other levels for that matter, can afford least of all to be isolated from the help and cooperation which Catholic sources can give them. These areas are, furthermore, basic to academic excellence.

In the over-all development of the college, and therefore also in the process of accreditation, the more important phases are in the formulation of the statement of purposes of the institution and the factual studies showing how well these purposes are being met. Within this evaluative framework, all other aspects of the institution must be considered. Thus, accrediting agencies, upon finding that the purposes of the college are clearly and intelligently described and that there is sufficient factual evidence on hand to indicate that they are being reasonably well attained, are willing to place their stamp of approval on such an institution. The key words here are "being reasonably well attained." The achievement may range anywhere from mere adequacy to excellence. But even should the degree of attainment be one of comparative excellence, there are many factors which require every college to study and review both purposes and outcomes on a continuing basis; changes in administration, teaching staff, the student body, certain subject-matter areas, teaching techniques, and our social and technological world in general can all have almost immediate direct or indirect effect upon the educational institution. Now such continuing study for the Catholic college certainly cannot be from a secular point of view, nor can Catholic educators be satisfied with only secular criteria in this regard. Even though an accrediting group makes every effort to understand the Catholic institution and its educational philosophy, it would seem apparent that it can do little by way of guiding such an institution to the needed greater achievement in those aspects which are and must be truly of a Catholic nature. Moreover, there are many different kinds of Catholic academic institutions, some of which are quite peculiar to Catholicism. Their uniqueness and complexity are frequently missed by the average secular evaluator. For example, in the field of higher education, in addition to the usual colleges for laymen and for laywomen or for both, there are colleges for the training of members of religious communities for women and the so-called major and minor seminaries for men. And within these groups there will be different types in order to train members not only for the religious life but also for some definite work of the community: nursing, teaching, social service, missionary fields, and others. Often our traditional emphasis on the liberal arts and the varying complexities which exist in both small Catholic colleges and larger universities are not clearly understood, as is evident by the tendency of some to consider Catholic education as one conforming whole, to be equated with a kind of academic inbreeding. The true influence of Catholic philosophy and Catholic educational thinking is not understood as being a stabilizing factor, while at the same time permitting a variety of proximate purposes and great flexibility in methods and techniques. These, then, are areas which must be, in the final analysis, the united concern of Catholic educators.

To pursue this thought even more concretely, let me give several examples. It is not uncommon for the non-Catholic evaluator to complain that a college program has too many courses in religion, including under this heading offerings in philosophy and theology as well as Church history. Such a criticism would indicate certainly a confused understanding of the college's objectives. Then too, some of the purposes of a Catholic college would have little appeal to some non-Catholic educators, such as certain characteristics of a good Catholic family life. Thus, related data on outcomes by way of the number of marriages and divorces among the alumni of the college, the birth rate of the Catholic college graduates, and other similar matters would be of comparatively little significance to them. Yet we Catholic educators should be especially sensitive to such information, considering it along with evidence of intellectual achievements, if our philosophy is to be truly meaningful and if our future progress is to be truly based on our philosophy.

Should the process of admission be any different for a Catholic college from that for any other kind of institution? In general, no! But every educational institution, while having aims in common with all others of its type, may reasonably be expected to have certain special objectives of its own. This is true, as I have already pointed out, of Catholic educational institutions. These differences, if taken seriously, will have an effect on admission requirements. Since the student body is in a constant state of flux, the correlation of admissions policies with outcomes is always a matter for constant study by college administrators, whether before or after accreditation. This need for study coupled with the close relationships of admissions policies to objectives indicates again the peculiar need of Catholic colleges for cooperation among themselves in solving certain admissions problems and in setting up their own evaluative machinery to do so. Our small institutions of higher education serving a single religious community are especially in need of answers to questions that constantly plague them: how to maintain satisfactory admissions standards for the prospective members of the community who will be expected to be successful in attaining the baccalaureate and higher degrees, while at the same time caring for the subjects whom the Lord did not endow with such intellectual powers but did bless with a solid religious vocation? Moreover, the seminary must seek one solution while religious orders of women may approach the problem by admitting such persons into the college in some limited status. But in all instances, the administrator has the never-ending responsibility to recognize and work honestly toward all the professed purposes of the college, seeking the advice of secular and other Catholic educators and agencies as the nature of the problem demands.

Another situation peculiar to Catholic colleges arises in connection with enrollment and finances. Every state of the union which has an active department of education has, until very recently, required a fixed enrollment of fifty, sometimes of one hundred students, before approval is given for the establishment of a junior or senior college. Such a policy originated in the principle that at minimum enrollment was needed to support the college financially.

If this standard were maintained strictly, some Catholic colleges throughout the land, especially those set up by small religious communities for their own members, could never be approved and in some localities would be forced out of existence. While greater flexibility is now in evidence, the very small college still comes under the influence of this quantitative standard. Non-Catholic professional educators must be constantly reminded that the practical reason for the establishment of this criterion does not actually exist in this kind of Catholic institution, that these colleges are supported by the treasury of the motherhouse of the religious community, not by funds obtained through tuition fees. Therefore, for them, the regulation has no validity. The entire area of finance within the Catholic college, moreover, is a difficult one in the eyes of these same people. The setting-up of accounting systems and their evaluation in terms of the over-all good and general welfare of the Catholic college can parallel in many ways the practices followed by their non-Catholic sister institutions. For their complete satisfactory development, however, there are aspects of "donated services," expenditures, and financial control that require specialized attention, attention that only experienced Catholics in the field can give.

Educators for many years have recognized certain broad criteria for determining the quality of teaching. It is generally accepted, however, that to state categorically the specific components of good teaching is not really possible, that the general criteria have validity only when viewed in the light of the locale in which the teaching takes place, that to attain their fullest sginificance these criteria must be applied by those who understand thoroughly the milieu which is involved. According to our Catholic philosophy of education, the concept of integration is vitally important as a factor of good teaching, and our concept of integration, which has philosophy and theology as core subjects, differs considerably from that of the secular educator. The academic integration problem, which is far from solved in many educational institutions, is therefore one of vital concern to the Catholic college, no matter what is its status of accreditation. It is, moreover, one that can seek solution only within the faculties of our own institutions, one that requires total effort from every Catholic educator and Catholic professional agency that is concerned with Catholic educational excellence. No other person or group of persons can solve this thorny problem for us.

Closely related to the problem of the quality of teaching are placement policies and practices. In the smaller Catholic boarding colleges, especially where a home-like atmosphere under the guidance of a religious community exists, the placing of students can be handled successfully in spite of a lack of classes and courses offered at the varying levels

usually deemed important to meet the needs of individual students. In a small, devoted group of
faculty members, permeated by a family spirit, private help and encouragement will often fill a gap
in the student's previous training and enable him to
proceed successfully in the regular class. The challenging of a superior student, under similar circumstances, can also be accomplished by individualized
attention in the classroom. Such an atmosphere may
even have implications for grading that would be
difficult for our own non-Catholic colleagues, attached to larger institutions, to recognize.

The curriculum is, of course, the heart of an
academic institution. Yet there is no such thing as
the "perfect" curriculum, one which may be judged
of such a quality that it may be considered "fixed"
for any specific period of time. On the contrary, the
program of studies, if it is to make a proper contribution to the advancement of the institution in this
age of never-ending changes in American life, must
be kept constantly under review. Since it makes the
major contribution to the attainment of the college's
objectives, it needs to be studied and reviewed by
those who have a thorough understanding of those
objectives. Accreditation or non-accreditation has
little or no direct relationship to this responsibility
of the college administrator. Unless this responsibility is whole-heartedly accepted by them at all times
and the Catholic aspects are given full consideration

in all subject fields, the institution soon will be paying mere lip-service to Catholic philosophy and
Catholic educational principles; it will be Catholic
in name only.

There are many examples of non-Catholic evaluators failing to understand many of the characteristics of Catholic programs of study, but perhaps
the most frequent misunderstanding which arises is
connected with the seminary college. To illustrate, I
shall recall one actual incident. A certain group of
men religious wished to have its college section (it
had gone over to 4-4-4 plan of organization for their
seminary) accredited by its regional association. The
evaluators were struck by the fact that only one
major field, namely, philosophy, was offered in the
college and asked among other similar questions the
following: "Must all students do their major work
in the field of philosophy? What do you do for those
students whose chief interests lie in other fields?"
The answer to these questions is very clear to the
Catholic. In the light of the purposes of this kind
of college, the training of young men for the priesthood, there is no place within its walls for a student
who is not greatly concerned with enhancing his
knowledge of philosophy. This is not only obscure to the non-Catholic, it is also difficult to
explain.

The extra curricular activities of a Catholic educational institution which are of a religious nature

will be ignored by secular educational advisers or at least not fully accepted. Since any degree of acceptance is generally the result of a careful explanation of the nature of their contribution to the attaining of the institution's purposes, it can hardly be expected that such individuals will be able to give profitable and sound advice for their continued development and general effectiveness. Here also the Catholic educator must keep in constant touch with the leadership in this field.

Personnel services have over the years presented a difficult problem for Catholic educational administrators. This has been due largely to the totally different concepts which Catholic and non-Catholic educators possess of the term. To the non-Catholic, personnel services have little if any connection with the students' private spiritual and religious problems. They are concerned by and large with helping the student adjust himself to the affairs of the world in the present and to help him prepare himself for the mundane surroundings into which he will be projected in the immediate future. Religious problems are not regarded strictly as a part of this activity. To the Catholic personnel officer all this is indeed important, and he accepts this as part of his responsibility. It is an activity which, if well carried on, will keep many matters from becoming so serious as to require confidential religious care. To the Catholic educator, personnel services are a truncated operation if they do not include, even though they are carried on strictly in a separate compartment by themselves, the religious care and attention which all Catholics feel that they as Catholics should seek and receive. How all this can best be carried on is by no means a rigidly established procedure. It involves many problems and still needs expert attention and study. Furthermore, it definitely requires a Catholic approach and direction. It can by no means be carried on in an isolated fashion, and least of all should it be influenced by the thinking of our non-Catholic friends who for the most part are influenced by an educational philosophy which would eliminate all teaching of a positive and sectarian religion.

The expression that the library is the heart of an educational institution has become bromidic, but it is still a deeply truthful statement. I have heard evaluators say that if they had only a half-hour within which to appraise an educational institution they would, with confidence in the results, spend it all in the library. There are so many aspects of the library, which reflect the qualities of essentially all other features of the institution. The collection of books in the philosophy and theology sections will, to be sure, tell much about the Catholic nature of the school or college, but almost of greater importance in this connection are the books in the other sections because they will throw light on the success with which the administration has solved that most difficult problem of the integration of all subjects of the curriculum with philosophy and theology. Progress toward the solution of this difficulty can be made only by a concerted effort by all Catholic educators and again should go on without interruption after whatever accreditation the institution has achieved.

I hope that even after this brief survey of some of the salient features in the development of a Catholic educational institution, the importance of a continuing study of its academic problems is evident. The never-ending process of improvement is common to all schools and colleges, Catholic and non-Catholic alike. Nor can any great distinction be made between the accredited and the non-accredited institution; the difference is only a relative one, each working at its particular level of development. What is important for Catholic educators to recognize is that precious element, pervading every facet of their institutions, which makes them Catholic and which requires intelligent fostering as long as their institutions continue to exist. There is no time in the growth of any educational institution when the authorities can afford to say: "We have reached our goal. We can now rest comfortably." The struggle for improvement must always go on, and surcease from it brings on an inevitable backward trend.

In this forward movement, all educational institutions, even the most reputedly best, need all possible help and support. The Catholic ones must rely and cooperate with the accepted accrediting groups of our ountry; they are a valuable and important part of the American system of education. They cannot afford to drift into academic isolation. But equally important, the Catholic institution must be developed as a Catholic institution in all its aspects. To do so systematically and fully, with economy of time and effort, their Catholic educational contacts must be maintained and enlarged, cultivated, and cherished, whether accreditation be a goal still sought or the first mile-stone already passed.

CHAPTER EIGHTEEN

COOPERATION IN CATHOLIC HIGHER EDUCATION

Cooperation among institutions of higher education throughout the United States, whether among Catholic or non-Catholic colleges and universities, has received serious consideration spasmodically over a long period, especially during periods of financial depression, when enrollments and endowments decline and many institutions are threatened with bankruptcy. The problem has recently been brought to the fore with renewed vigor through the efforts of the Sister Formation Movement to strengthen the many small colleges of religious communities of women which have opened in such great numbers. Little, however, has been accomplished of a lasting nature toward this end within Catholic circles, although much has been done among our non-Catholic brethren.

Cooperation is not to be confused in this discussion with amalgamation. In the great furor which has been roused in recent years over this general question, the two have been confused and even regarded as synonymous, causing much misunderstanding and some heat. Let it be understood from the start that in spite of all the talk among Catholic educators about the desirability of our colleges pooling their resources, even to the extent of making one institution out of several, we are still of the firm opinion that, all factors considered, we do not have enough Catholic colleges to meet the needs of the Church and of the country. This does not mean, however, that Catholic higher education cannot profit from much well-considered cooperation, and it is this subject strictly that we propose to discuss here.

Powerful forces militate in general against any extensive cooperation among institutions of higher learning. It is well that we consider these before we proceed to the more constructive portions of our discussion.

In the judgment of many educators the greatest obstacle to greater cooperation is narrow institutionalism. Institutionalism has been defined as "the attitude of devotion and loyalty to a single school which springs from some cause other than excellence in the performance of legitimate educational functions." It has its origin in local ambitions and jealousies and in a sentimental rather than in a well thought out plan for the future. It appears also in the sentimental attachment of alumni which brings them to the attitude of "My alma mater, right or wrong." Unfortunately many college teachers feel that they fall short of their full duty to the college, unless they instill this unreasoned attitude into the minds of all students with whom they come in contact. It usually passes under the name of "college spirit." On the other hand, it is not necessary for a teacher to be chronically disgruntled. It should be possible for him to have a calm, dispassionate attitude toward matters of such great importance to him as those of his college.

Another major obstacle to cooperation in higher education, probably second only to institutionalism, is plain ignorance of the importance of the problem on the part of the controlling boards, administrative officers, faculties, educational organizations, the constituencies of the institutions, and the general public. This point could be discussed at great length. Examples in support of this statement are numerous. A prominent member of a regional accrediting association once said: "Board (trustees) members in my region are ignorant of higher education practices, unduly conservative, and afflicted with inertia, procrastination, and prejudice." This statement is obviously an exaggeration, but certainly anyone who has dealt very extensively with these groups cannot say that it is entirely without foundation. Several presidents and deans, with apparent sincerity, have with some embarrassment stated in public that they know so little and have thought so much less about relations with their institutional neighbors that they can give no information and express no intelligent opinions on institutional cooperation. Even more to be deplored are those college and university administrators who, although situated in a small area well populated with institutions of higher education, declare that they are entirely free of the problem; they have no need for cooperation and coordination.

The influence of special purpose and pressure groups is known to all administrators of colleges and universities, but probably best to the administrative officers of state institutions. This phase of the topic will not be discussed here. But we may be justified in mentioning at this point the determination on the part of some religious communities to set up colleges in the vicinity of other Catholic colleges not because they are convinced that they can contribute something to Catholic higher education in the region and not because of a carefully considered plan, but simply because "our boys or our girls want us to open a college and will support us." Private philanthropy in some instances also has resulted in educational and financial lack of cooperation. Catholic educational institutions have thus far received comparatively little favorable attention from the philanthropic but enough to have experienced some of its disadvantages. Wealthy industrialists have left large bequests to higher educational institutions with the provision that the recipient institution establish or enlarge some designated department. Few institutions have refused such windfalls and proceed to set up departments and services already amply provided by neighboring institutions.

According to college and university administrators the alumni represent easily the most vociferous group in protesting cooperative effort. Contrary to common opinion, their influence and interests extend beyond the realm of athletics. A university with which I am well acquainted proposed several years ago to abandon its school of law, which was accumulating a large annual deficit, on the ground that this field was amply provided for by several neighboring institutions and the attention and money spent on this school might be used to better advantage on other activities more closely associated with its professed purposes. The alumni of the school protested vigorously on the ground that the university should not subject them to the disgrace of having received a law degree from a defunct school. The law school, moreover, because of the protest was continued in spite of all the attendant disadvantages, and continues annually to contribute a considerable deficit to the university.

The question has sometimes been raised regarding the possibility and the desirability of cooperation between Catholic and non-Catholic institutions of higher education. It is obvious that fundamental differences in basic philosophy constitute a serious obstacle to the development of such cooperation. It is equally obvious that Catholic institutions may not join with non-Catholic groups in any common project in which there might even appear to be any compromise in the fundamental doctrines of the Church. This phase of the question is a very delicate one, but some form of cooperation, if only in a restricted manner, does seem possible.

Racial and national prejudice, all equally indefensible in the Church and in a democracy of the American kind, are undoubtedly serious obstacles to the development of greater cooperation among higher institutions. While it is true that the Church in America has seen fit to establish a very small number of educational institutions for the benefit of a special race, it is a pity that the need to set up these few was ever felt. National groups on the other hand, in spite of the willingness of colleges and universities to offer their resources for the general training of the youth of these groups, have had a tendency to set up their own institutions, stressing the culture of the old fatherland. The institutions of higher education under Catholic auspices already established should be able to provide, especially with ordinary cooperation, for the needs of all races and the peoples of all nationalistic origins as well. It is the belief of many that racial and nationalistic antagonisms are becoming less of an obstacle with the years in the movement toward cooperation. Fortunately, this seems indeed to be true.

Within recent years, ever since the inauguration of the Sister Formation Movement, some indignation has been roused over the rapid and extensive foundation of novitiate institutions, both of the two-year and four-year kind, by religious communities for the training of their own prospective members. This matter deserves serious and thorough treatment, but we are concerned here only with the element of cooperation. It is true that there exists a strong willingness among these communities to help other religious and to cooperate with them in the training of their subjects, but at best this can be only on a temporary basis. The considerations that bring this about are the following: Every religious community has its own plan on how its members should be trained, and believes firmly that it alone can do the job. Even within the groups which follow the same rule, each has its own thoughts on how the rule can best be inculcated in its subjects. Each will have differences of opinion as to which phases of the rule should receive greater or less emphasis. Furthermore, nearly all religious communities, although willing out of Christian charity to help struggling groups in the training of future members by receiving them into the classes of their own novitiate colleges, regard these externs essentially as interlopers, and quite naturally look forward to the time when these visitors will have their own training centers.

Other obstacles to cooperation may be mentioned briefly. Political influence has permeated many institutions, both public and private, so as to interfere greatly with efforts to cooperate, both within and without. Political considerations involved in the appointments of members of governing boards and presidents may sometimes extend to favorite candidates for deans and faculty members. This is true in private and even denominational institutions but it is most frequently noted in state and municipal colleges and universities. Another obstacle to cooperation both between institutions and even within a single institution is personal ambition. It is the personal and selfish ambition of both administrative officers and faculty members to glorify themselves and improve or safeguard their economic status. Most administrators are very reluctant about taking any steps that might result in their institution's being consolidated with others, thus making necessary only one administrative staff instead of two. Similarly, faculty members try to retain their courses and to develop them into separate departments, schools, or colleges within a university, with themselves in the higher position of professor, department head, or even dean. Thus, departments and courses expand and multiply rather than become more correlated. In the process, needless duplication arises and dead wood is found everywhere. All this leads to narrow institutionalism with unfair student recruiting, superficial loyalty, and all their attendant evils.

Many real and imaginary administrative difficulties may be regarded as obstacles to greater cooperation both within and without educational institutions. For example, classes may be scheduled at different times and in different ways; extra-curricular activities, controlled by tradition, may interfere; and so on. But these difficulties are for the most part details which are by no means insurmountable. More serious administrative problems are: distances and transportation facilities between campuses, differences in curriculum, one emphasizing one phase of the work, and one another, different entrance requirements and differences in fees, often occasioned by varying financial support; the adjustment of graduate and undergraduate programs. But these difficulties also may be overcome.

Various types of legal problems may interfere with greater cooperation. The type with which Catholic institutions are chiefly concerned arises from the restrictions that are sometimes imposed by the charters or acts of incorporation under which private institutions operate. But even charters and acts of incorporation can be changed if the will and the patience to bring this about exist. Most administrators are very reluctant to bring up any matter relating to the charter of their institutions for fear that in so doing some special features and privileges may be rescinded.

These are probably the most serious obstacles to increased cooperation among Catholic institutions of higher education. Some of these can be removed or at least reduced rather easily, while others obviously require a long and slow treatment. But to say that any of them are entirely insurmountable is certainly not the part of a forceful and forward-looking university or college administration.

The agencies of influence which may work to overcome the obstacles to cooperation in higher education and effect at least a greater degree of successful common planning are many, but, it must be admitted, they have thus far been rather ineffective. Some Catholics have an apparently simple solution to all the difficulties herein concerned. Let the members of the hierarchy demand cooperation at least among the institutions of their own dioceses and we will at once produce it in full bloom. This is the general trend of their thinking, which corresponds somewhat to that of some non-Catholics who would rely on the powers of the state to do the same thing. The solution of the problem, I fear, is not as easy as that. The members of the American hierarchy can do much in this matter, of course, and they probably represent the most potent agency within Catholic circles for overcoming the obstacles just discussed, but to be really successful in their efforts they must have the support of other forces, especially the good will of Catholic educators themselves and thinking Catholics generally. Simply the forceful demand for cooperation in higher education by whatever authority will not achieve it at its best, and the members of the American hierarchy seem thus far to have appreciated this thoroughly.

Other agencies, which deserve at least a brief mention, may be classed as national, regional, and state. There is, of course, no national body, either public or private, that exercises control over the development of higher education as a uniform national enterprise. There are, however, a number of agencies, both public and private, that exercise a considerable degree of control and influence of a nation-wide character over specific aspects and phases of higher educational life. Some of these are: the United States Office of Education, the Department of Education of The National Catholic Welfare Conference, functioning much as does the United States Office of Education and sometimes in cooperation with it; the National Education Association; the National Catholic Educational Association; the

Association of American Universities; the American Council on Education; the Association of American Colleges; and others. These groups may well contribute much to cooperation in higher education. Some of them have attacked the problem directly. No one of them has accomplished a great deal. Learned societies and educational foundations represent strong potential forces of national character for cooperation in research, although they fall far short of their potentialities in actual accomplishment.

Regional and state kinds of agencies which promote cooperation among institutions of higher education are similar to the national ones. Usually, they are subdivisions of the national organization. I need mention only those established under the Smith-Hughes Act to promote and guide vocational education, for example, instruction in home economics. An agency of this kind, by refusing its recognition, could do much to break down the separatist tendencies of individuals and institutions. The only regional groups under Catholic auspices which might take on a similar power for good in a constructive way are the regional sections of the National Catholic Educational Association and, corresponding somewhat to the state groups, diocesan educational organizations. The Sister Formation group can, of course, be a great influence in this direction with Catholic colleges for women.

Cooperation among different Catholic institutions is possible in many ways. We can do no more here than mention a few. Reference has already been made to cooperation in research among institutions of higher education. In spite of the popular notion that good teaching and scientific research are incompatible, many still believe that not only training in research but continued development in scientific investigation is most advantageous for improvement in teaching. However, be that as it may, the fact remains that the faculties of our Catholic colleges contain literally hundreds of individuals, well trained for genuine research. Certainly, there must be enough leadership among our scholars to organize these individuals for research projects of genuine importance in different fields. This in my opinion would not only improve teaching but would raise the intellectual level of our institutions of higher education.

Teachers may well be exchanged or shared. It is sometimes desirable to offer courses in certain fields only every other year. In alternate years the instructor might well be employed by a neighboring institution, thus eliminating the necessity of an additional instructor. Or an instructor may not be required to offer a full-time program in his subject in his own institution and so will be able to give some service to another simultaneously. Something by way of an interchange of instructors has been going on among our colleges chiefly in summer sessions. While this is advantageous in many respects, it lacks, because of its temporary character, much of the nature of the cooperation about which we are speaking.

Every college must be expected to give efficient instruction in all subjects considered as basic for a liberal or, as some would have it today, general education. But it is impossible for a small college to offer advanced courses or facilities for genuine concentration in all basic fields, to say nothing of the less important subjects. Some kind of distribution of the fields of concentration might well be arranged between institutions within comparatively easy commuting distance. Physical facilities for advanced study in certain fields, especially in the natural sciences, are very costly. There scarely seems to be any necessity for duplicating costly equipment among such institutions. Specialization in institutional development with respect to certain physical facilities might well be arranged between neighboring institutions.

On the side of the graduate school, certain fields of research should by reason of their general importance and universality be developed as efficiently as possible in all universities, e.g. philosophy, psychology, and English. But other departments might well be confined to one or two universities in the entire country, e.g. Semitic languages and literatures, Slavic languages and literatures, and seismology. Even within a single field, subdivisions of the subject might well be assigned to specific universities for intensive development.

Similarly two graduate schools under Catholic auspices could very advantageously join in the supervision of the research and study by students under certain circumstances. Non-Catholic institutions do this rather frequently. I have yet to find a definite instance of this among Catholic graduate schools.

Much is said today, especially at meetings of national learned societies, regarding post-doctoral research. A student who has completed his work for the doctorate finds himself in the midst of much material which should be investigated at once. Sometimes the material will lose its value or the investigation will have little significance, if not carried through immediately. Such projects are often organized as joint institutes of post-doctoral research. Catholic educators may well consider doing likewise. Similarly the joint maintenance of clearinghouse facilities for research, bibliographical resources, publication, and various academic services, while becoming more common daily among our non-Catholic neighbors, are rarely even discussed among the scholars of our Catholic institutions of higher education.

If institutions in the same general region are devoting their chief attention to distinctly different objectives, they may still cooperate effectively in recruiting or in the joint presentation of the educational advantages afforded by the group. They may even cooperate in fund campaigns.

Cooperative sponsoring of special programs of fine arts, music, drama, and lectures seem clearly beneficial and easily effected, yet almost never carried out. It is quite non-existent in athletic and sports activities.

It would be ludicrous indeed, were the results not so tragic, to see two Catholic institutions within the same city limits, spending thousands of dollars to establish departments or schools of advanced nursing or of library science or of any other professional subjects. Difficulties may be raised about distributing opportunities for concentration in the so-called fundamental fields, but it should be easy for colleges to agree on an equitable distribution of the various professions which exist to some extent as independent units.

It is difficult also to justify the duplication by Catholic institutions of programs of extension and adult education. Opportunities for self-improvement could be greatly expanded for the adult by a little cooperative planning.

Before closing my remarks on this subject, I would like to make my position clear on two points about which it may be wrongly judged. First, I do not believe that we have too many Catholic colleges in the land, not even that we have too many Catholic colleges for women in any one locality. If the Catholic population of any given district be examined, as well as the nature of the non-Catholic people of that area who might be inclined to send their children to Catholic institutions, no condition will be found so bad that it cannot be remedied by a little cooperation. Instead of entering upon a program of rivalry, these institutions should plan through cooperation to do the best possible job of offering Catholic higher education in that particular area. Actually, all things considered, we need more Catholic colleges both for men and for women in almost every part of our country, provided that some systematic plan of cooperation can be adopted.

Second, my conviction is strong not only that a well-planned scheme of cooperation among Catholic colleges and universities would be a great boon to Catholic education and the work of the Church, but that all the obstacles which I have mentioned above can be overcome in order to attain it. In fact, I am sure that if Catholic educators set out to establish some worthwhile scheme of cooperation, they will receive strong support on every hand. My one serious concern is that of the proper leadership for such important movements. The initiative and leadership must be such as will inspire the confidence of all concerned—the educators themselves, the religious superiors, the members of the hierarchy. Finally, it must be remembered that cooperation is not a panacea for all the ills of Catholic higher education. It can, however, be very helpful.

CHAPTER NINETEEN

THE ADVISABILITY OF A SUMMER SESSION

Fifty or more years ago when summer sessions first came into existence, they were very much like the Chautauqua assemblies of the period, combining lectures and entertainments of various kinds and often held outdoors. They might even be called intellectual vacations. Naturally, opposition arose immediately in educational circles to accepting academic credits by transfer when earned under such conditions. Gradually the extreme entertainment features were abolished by institutions of higher education, and more and more insistence was placed on serious study. Furthermore, it became increasingly evident that a regular session of the institution of higher education during the summer months was badly needed for several reasons. Students, who during the regular semesters had failed a course or more, wished for an opportunity to make up this work and thus keep up with their classes. Some, especially teachers, found it practically impossible to give up teaching during the regular year in order to finish the requirements for a degree, and they were looking for some way to complete the work for a bachelor's degree and in recent years especially for the master's degree during the off season. Others were anxious to accelerate during the summer the completion of a regular program, especially in times of national emergency. Still others, not interested in a degree but wishing to increase their competence for teaching various subjects, could find this opportunity in the summer months alone. Thus the summer session as a period for serious study rapidly came into being, and earned the respect of all educators. The only feature of the original Chatauqua-like summer terms still retained by modern summer sessions is that of furnishing an opportunity for an intellectual vacation, as it were. Persons of cultivated taste seek ways and means of improving themselves intellectually, and usually are able to do this only during the summer season. In fact, they well might not be accepted as students, in particular as candidates for degrees, in the regular semesters. This practice is regarded today by the administrators of our leading institutions of higher education as a very worthy activity for summer sessions, to serve this class of students.

Some institutions of higher education have organized their summer work into another semester or quarter, according to the general arrangement of their calendar. This can be done advantageously only if the constituents of the institution concerned are following a schedule of work and study which will enable them to attend a regular session during the summer. Experience has shown that this is not possible in some parts of the country, e.g., the East, North-East, and Far-West, where the activities of the regular year overlap into the early part of the summer and begin in the very early fall. When, however, this arrangement is possible, the summer session presents no problem. It is simply another regular term or semester of the institution. Most colleges and universities cannot make the adjustments in their calendars so as to permit giving a regular third term. Such a change would interfere directly with the regularly scheduled activities of those whom the institutions are primarily endeavoring to serve and thus clash with the very purpose of their existence.

The most common length of the summer session for all practical purposes is six weeks. On the other hand, some Catholic colleges, by no means those of the highest academic standing, attempt to squeeze a program into a period of five weeks which will yield the same number of semester-hours of credit as would normally be obtained in a six-weeks session. This is done by increasing the class hours to the proper number without any thought of the number of clock hours of study necessary for a student to earn genuine college credits in that period. Both the shortness of the period and certain peculiar purposes of the summer session make it imperative that a special officer be appointed to take the over-all responsibility for its smooth running and success. All the details of administration for the various divisions or schools of a complex organization or the several departments of an institution of simple organization must be established as a close unit, so that the summer session can start promptly with as little loss of time as possible and proceed to the end smoothly. This is important because in a six-weeks summer session only the very minimum number of class-hours regularly required for a semester hour of credit is feasible, unless the class hours are arranged in a very irregular manner. This is not possible unless there is a great abundance of classrooms, which usually is not the case. Thus no time of the regular classes should be lost because of the failure to organize properly beforehand and the necessity of making adjustments after the session has started. Only the person responsible for the entire operation can do this. Only he knows all the various activities of the summer session, and when and where they will take place. Also, because of the nature of the summer session, many will be attending class who belong to no particular school or division of the institution, and will have to be allocated to some official of a dean's status. This is regularly the Director or Dean of the Summer Session. Furthermore, in planning the program of the summer session, the director by working with the various deans and heads of departments whose personnel is participating in the session, will have little difficulty in making his plans to this extent, but there will be much additional planning affecting a number of departments which he alone can and should be authorized to do. The summer session is an excellent place and time for inaugurating and testing possible new programs for the regular year. What these programs should be comes normally under the purview of the director or dean of the summer session. This kind of planning requires especially the attention of a well qualified person who has both the time necessary to give to it and the authority to carry it through. Again the budget of the summer session should be the responsibility of one person, the director or dean of the summer session. Although he will receive much assistance from the various regular deans and heads of departments, no one of these can very well be made responsible for the entire budget. All these reasons are enough to make it clear that an over-all administrative officer such as a director or dean is necessary for that academic unit known as the summer session, and that this academic period cannot be carried on advantageously by the administrative apparatus of the regular year alone.

By and large, the summer session has the same objectives as the regular terms, and naturally there should be close relationship between their respective programs. However, some of the possible special purposes of a summer session have just been mentioned. A careful statement of the purposes of the summer session, taking into consideration the local situation, is strongly advised, in which the general purposes as they coincide with those of the regular term should be depicted, as well as the special objectives as they contribute to the general aims of the institution.

All generalizations have certain weaknesses in that certain very peculiar and unusual circumstances are not accounted for. Although I am quite aware of this, I venture to make the following general statements with regard to the summer session. If the director is working closely with the academic deans and heads of departments, and if the director or dean is wide-awake to the special opportunities of the summer session for introducing new courses and new programs, the enrollment of the summer session should exceed to some extent the enrollments of the regular semesters. If this is not true, it is a fair assumption that the summer session is not being conducted according to its highest potentiality.

The question as to how much work accomplished during the summer sessions should be accepted as fulfilling the requirements for a bachelor's degree is having less and less significance as the quality of the studies in summer sessions is being continually raised. The tendency is to regard the summer session, at least that of one's own institution, as offering work of a quality on a par with that of the regular year, and in such instances naturally the question before us now has no validity. However, the feeling that work in summer sessions is necessarily inferior in quality to that of the regular sessions still persists in many quarters, and a limit as to the amount of this work taken in summer sessions which may be accepted toward a college degree is set rather low. This supposedly is a means of checking any serious undermining of the academic standards of the regular year. This limit is usually arbitrarily placed at a maximum of sixty semester hours.

All in all, it seems that any institution of higher education is not meeting its full obligation to the area which it serves, unless it does carry on a summer program Properly organized and carried out, it will prove an invaluable asset in connection with the institution's policy with regard to public relations. Finally, may I call attention to an oft-repeated axiom in the field of higher education: "The more an educational institution lets its roots down into the people of its general surroundings, the stronger it will become, and *vice versa*, the more an institution isolates itself and withdraws into a kind of ivory tower, the faster it will descend into oblivion." A live and active summer session will contribute much to the institution's enthusiastic reception by its immediate constituents, and can even prove to be a feeder to the institution in general.

CHAPTER TWENTY

WORKSHOPS

The workship technique has been enjoying ever increasing favor among educators ever since it was first introduced into the summer sessions more than a generation ago. The American Council on Education gave the initial impetus to the movement and sustained it in its early days. The original concept of the workshop technique was definitely a contribution to teaching procedures, and fortunately this has been maintained to a conspicuous extent. But unfortunately the term "workshop" has come to be applied more and more to educational activities of long standing far removed from the true workshop idea, and this practice has tended to obscure its original meaning in the minds of many and has, I believe, degraded the educational significance of the workshop in the popular mind.

A simple general definition of a workshop may be said to be the following: A group of people with extended experience in teaching or administration within a given field, who have gathered under the direction of specialists to discuss with others of similar experience the problems which they have encountered and for which they seek solutions. By its very definition, the workshop is a very important activity of any worthy institution of higher education.

The following kinds of educational gatherings have been and still are erroneously called workshops:

(1) Any gathering of a short duration from several hours to several days, open essentially to anyone who wishes to attend and characterized by a more or less directed open discussion has in recent years been called a workshop. Of course, this is far from the carefully planned and directed procedure of the real workshop. Strangely enough large and supposedly well-informed educational groups, such as the National Catholic Educational Association and the Middle States Association of Colleges and Secondary Schools have fallen into this error. The characteristics of open discussion seem to be about all that these gatherings have in common

with genuine workshops. These meetings might all be classified under the general title of conferences, and a term rarely used of late, symposiums.

(2) There is a temptation also on the part of some educators to single out the seminar portion of the workshop and concentrate on this one activity, labeling it a workshop. This is not so far off the track as will become evident a little later. A genuine seminar with several slight modifications could well result in an excellent workshop. Unfortunately some study groups, which do not even remotely approach the nature of a true seminar, are actually called seminars. The term "seminar" itself is subject to grave misunderstanding and abuse.

Persons of experience in organizing workshops may differ as to the amount of emphasis to be placed on the various phases of a workshop, but I think that they would agree on the essential ingredients that go to make a successful workshop. These ingredients are: lectures, discussions, and seminars. My own approach to the organization of a workshop has been as follows: The mornings are given more to a series of lectures followed by discussions on general topics, which taken together will cover the entire broad picture of a workshop's title. Several problems raise their heads here. While it is desirable for the record and the published proceedings that the lectures be written out, the delivery should be as informal as possible. Participants should be encouraged to break in and ask questions as circumstances seem to warrant. After the lecture has been delivered and after a brief recess of about ten minutes, the general discussion should be opened. This discussion may be allowed to take its natural course or it may be directed by questions formulated before the lecture and distributed among the audience. This is not meant to freeze the discussion but rather to stimulate it. The discussion should be permitted to proceed as the person in charge sees fit. Ordinarily it should not be allowed to continue for more than an hour. Experience has shown that beyond that point ideas are repeated and interest lags.

Lectures with discussions may be arranged for the evening also. They are to be distinguished from those of the morning by the fact that they are usually open to the public and not only to the regular participants in the workshop. Furthermore, the topics presented and discussed will have more wide-spread appeal, although appropriate to the workshop as announced, and may even be of some national importance. Otherwise, they will be conducted in the same manner as those scheduled for the morning hours.

The heart of the workshop is the seminars or the small discussion groups. I have usually scheduled those for the afternoon. They last for about two hours and may continue even longer if all concerned are willing. Among the items of information furnished by the participant before final registration is the nature of the problem or problems with which he is especially concerned. On the basis of this information, as well as by specific request, participants are assigned to the individual seminars. It often happens that one or more seminars will grow exceedingly large. These, of course, should be broken up into several divisions of the same seminar. The problem then arises of procuring adequate seminar leaders for the newly formed groups. The enrollment of the seminars should not be permitted to grow beyond twenty, preferably fifteen. If the preliminary data furnished by participants indicates that certain individuals do not properly fit into any existing seminar, an attempt should be made to organize additional groups. If this be found to be impracticable, the applicant should be informed of the situation, and, if possible be persuaded to accept enrollment in one of the existing seminars or to withdraw from the workshop entirely, as he may wish. Of course, if appropriate consultants can be found, the prospective participant may be urged to enroll in any existing seminar of his choice, and be promised direction on his particular problem from a specially appointed adviser.

A seminar may by reason of an overly enthusiastic leader very easily descend into another series of lectures or because of a lackadaisical director into aimless and undirected discussions. This is to be avoided at all costs. The success of the seminar groups and of the general conference depends upon the contributions of both leader and participants. Both must work together toward the realization of the values outlined as the objectives of the workshop.

The following statement of some of the responsibilities of the leaders and of the participants of a workshop have been adapted in part from an instruction sheet issued by the United States Office of Education.

I. Responsibilities of the Leader

1. *The persistent task* of the leader is to guide the discussion toward the solution of the problem at hand.

2. *The immediate task* of the leader is to shape conditions so that friendly, democratic relationships are established.

3. *The function* of the leader is to provide such an atmosphere as will stimulate and encourage the others to make their fullest contributions.

4. Sincere interest must be shown by the leader in what each person says.

5. The leader must guide the discussion so that there is a full, free interchange of opinion and thought.

6. The leader should endeavor to see that each participant has a background of knowledge which will enable him to make relevant contributions to

the discussion. Many will have this as the result of greater or less experience. Others will have to procure this, at least in part, by intensive reading at the moment. The leader should indicate what reading will be most helpful for this immediate purpose. All, regardless of experience, may well profit from this reading.

7. In leading a discussion the following points will prove helpful:

a. A clear statement of the problem is vital. The entire group should participate in this.

b. If the problem is a comprehensive one, less difficulty will be experienced if it is broken down into sub-problems.

c. Only relevant contributions will be considered. In rejecting irrelevant suggestions, however, the personality of the individual must be respected. The leader and the participants must do nothing which will cause a member of the group to "lose face."

d. Make sure that one point is finished before passing on to another.

e. Most leaders and participants find the outlining of major points on the black-board useful.

II. Responsibilities of the Participants

1. The participants must share the responsibility with the leader for the success or failure of the project.

2. The participants must be faithful and even enthusiastic about completing all the readings assigned by the leader.

3. There should be willingness on the part of the more articulate members to encourage the others to talk.

4. The group can function well only as each member freely shares his ideas.

5. The group will progress only as each member graciously and voluntarily subjects his ideas to the critical thinking of the others and to the test of facts.

6. An open-minded, objective attitude toward the experiences and opinions of the others is vital.

7. As each individual increasingly identifies his own purpose with group purposes, the group develops a strong unity and coherence.

8. When the leader and the participants honestly give their best, the ultimate satisfaction comes with the recognition that the final solution of the problem represents the combined thinking of all.

9. To help participants and leaders understand the emotional problems that often arise in a workshop, the following psychological factors are presented:

a. It is difficult for most people to feel free in situations where a number of people with differences in training and experience work together toward common goals.

b. The leaders and conference participants have to work together to provide this security for all conference members. Some ways of doing this are:

(1) To make sure that each person participating is recognized as an individual with a contribution to make which is important because he alone can make it.

(2) To assume that each person is making his contribution sincerely in the light of his best understanding.

(3) To receive all suggestions from group members with appreciation.

It is of vital importance that every member of a seminar have sufficient background through experience and possibly through reading to take an intelligent part and make some contribution in the discussions. Thus it behooves the Director of the Workshop to screen prospective participants carefully. He will be annoyed by persons who have had little or no experience in the field and essentially no knowledge of it, who for any one of a number of reasons will endeavor to be admitted to the workshop, and to obtain thereby at least the appearance of having received some training in the field. This brings us to the mechanism of administration.

First of all, at least several months before the opening of the workshop, a pamphlet should be produced and widely disseminated in appropriate places describing in detail the theme and plan of the project. It should contain the names and functions of all connected with it, also a sketch of all the resources available for the workshop. This pamphlet should include in detachable form two application forms: one for admission to the workshop, requesting all necessary information for passing on the request; the other for living accommodations, also requesting the needed data for intelligent processing.

A deadline should be set for filing these applications and, if circumstances dictate, strictly adhered to. This procedure will first of all enable the director to determine whether or not the demand for and interest in the workshop are sufficient to warrant going through with it. This will also make it possible for him to make the necessary additional divisions of a seminar and even to eliminate a seminar entirely if essentially no interest has been exhibited in it. Living accommodations, which are so important for the success of any workshop, can thus be cared for systematically and efficiently. Of course, there are countless other details which will have to be cared for as they arise and which it would serve no purpose to mention here. There are, however, several other important matters which should receive some attention.

Participants, once they have been admitted should be properly placed. Are they in the proper seminar in relation to the problem which they have brought with them for solution? In this connection at least one hour a day, or more if need be, should be set aside for special consultation with the director and his aides. This will be especially helpful in the early stages of a workshop. There is always some misunderstanding and misinterpretation on the part of prospective participants of the preliminary information given them.

The registration of participants should be made as simple and as little time-consuming as possible. Nothing can be more stimulating to a workshop than getting off to a fast start. There should be little difficulty here, if the two application forms mentioned above are used skillfully. The participant, when registering, should be obliged to do little more than sign in and pay his bill.

Should academic credit be given for successful attendance at a workshop? Ideally, the answer is: "No!" Ordinarily a workshop consists of a group of people who have long since passed the stage of struggling for a degree. They have been active in the field for some years and their chief concern is to get help toward the solution of the problems which they have met in those years. Actually, however, with the American educational world enmeshed in credits of all kinds as a measure of one's fitness for almost any position in the field of education, the pressure to request and to grant credits for workshop experience is great indeed. The granting or withholding of academic credit is one of the greatest administrative problems in the area of the workshop. There has been much abuse here to the discredit of the workshop technique. When the clock hours spent at a workshop are gathered from every possible source and this total is divided by fifteen to determine the number of semester hours of credit to be granted, as is frequently done, workshop directors are making a mockery of workshop administration. It reminds one of many mechanical procedures of the business world.

It is also my strong conviction that any workshop which is at all worthwhile should have its proceedings published. These should include not only the lectures but also whatever is of any importance which may have emerged from the discussions, and the important results of the deliberations of the seminar.

Finally, may I say once more that there is no fixed mechanical procedure to be followed in every workshop. The one unchangeable feature is the seminar. Unless the integrity of the seminar, as I have described it, is maintained there is no true workshop. All other activities such as the lectures and discussions, informal gatherings and debates, are supplementary. They are intended to refurbish the seminars, and the extent and the manner in which they are used are variable and depend on the nature of the subject of the workshop and on the quality of the workshop's participants.

Of the desirability, if not the necessity, for any worthwhile college or university including true workshop activity in its over-all program, there can be no doubt. As I have shown above, a very important group of persons are reached, who could not be affected in any other way.

CHAPTER TWENTY-ONE

ADULT EDUCATION

Probably the greatest stumbling block to the general acceptance of Adult Education as a dignified and serious division of general education is the prevailing notion that it consist of teaching anything to adults that adults wish to learn, without holding them to any qualitative level of achievement. All persons concerned with the administration of adult education are agreed that no academic credit should be given for any courses in the field, however faithfully completed. This seems to be the only feature of adult education on which all educators essentially agree. Yet this principle by itself gives very little substantive quality to adult education.

As to the nature of the subject matter taught in this field, I would add two qualifications to the general description of adult education just made. The work given in the division of adult education must at least be a challenge to the average adult mentally, or to his I.Q., if you prefer, and also must be dignified and worthy of a person of average mentality and respectability. These limitations would eliminate such things as teaching how to play golf, make ice-cream, play games of chances, and run a numbers racket.

Attempts have been made to recognize several different kinds of adult education, e.g. parochial, diocesan, academic, and recreational. We are appropriately concerned here with academic adult education, that is adult education carried on by regularly established academic institutions, in particular, institutions of higher education. While I would by no means eliminate the secondary school completely as a center of adult education, I believe that there are in general a number of considerations that argue distinctly against the secondary school as the most desirable location for this work. First of all, we cannot escape the fact that we are for the most part dealing with adults and not teenagers, and the association of the secondary school with adolescents will tend to be displeasing and unattractive to adults. Then, too, the secondary school will not have the resources, especially in personnel, to offer the program of studies usually in demand by adults. It might even be added that the adaptation of secondary school teaching procedures to the requirements of adult education classes is a much more difficult process than the similar one with respect to college and university teaching.

Adult education, if it is to have a worthy academic status, should aim to promote the intellectual interests and developments of adults, and should indeed not be hampered in its efforts to achieve this end by such things as the usual admission requirements and prerequisites, examinations, fixed subject matter and of the other accouterments of formal education. Moreover, with the enrollment of the class membership being, all in all, quite unpredictable and usually very varied, the teacher must be prepared to adapt his subject matter and his teaching procedures even at the last moment according to the students in his class. On the other hand, the teacher must not deal with trivialities or matter in general unworthy of an adult's time and attention.

Adult education is not only quite appropriate as an activity of a true institution of higher education, including even a university in the best sense of the word, but very important for its future well-being. The great danger to any institution of higher learning, and especially to those which have been established by genuine scholars on the basis of the highest scholarly principles, is that it will develop in a rarified atmosphere of pure science and nothing else, or, worse still, in surroundings of intellectual snobbery, and gradually find itself in a vacuum, completely cut off from its time and from the people of the region in which it exists. Such colleges and universities can only wither and die, and the history of higher education is strewn with their remains. The beginnings of universities in Europe, and of higher education in this country, in particular Johns Hopkins University, The Catholic University of America, Clark University, and the University of Chicago were founded with the conviction that these institutions were necessarily to be joined intimately with the needs and the requirements of the lives of the people surrounding them. By placing their roots here they would draw to themselves the nourishment and support so vital to their existence. A well planned and directed program of adult education is one of the most efficacious means available to any educational institution for the establishment of this life-giving relationship, and, while its headquarters and general management belong in the college or university, it must be ready to carry on anywhere, wherever it can best reach the people who need its benefits.

Therefore, to do its work thoroughly, Catholic adult education should proceed according to the demands of the moment from the institutions of higher education to the parish hall, or to the classrooms of a grade school or a high school building, or even to private homes; but, in order to succeed best, it must be directed by persons of broad intellectual background and experience, such as are usually found in true institutions of higher learning. The British trade unions appreciated this when, just before the period of World War II, they approached the authorities of Oxford and Cambridge universities for advice and support (which incidentally were granted them with genuine enthusiasm) in conducting adult education programs.

It is almost a bromide to state that adult education is the continuation of a person's intellectual training and to a certain degree the further development of his skills after the formal period of his education and training has ceased. There are, at the one extreme, adults who, despite the compulsory education laws of the country, have never attended school long enough to learn how to read and write acceptably. On the other hand, men and women of the professions,—lawyers, doctors, and even members of the clergy may well desire to take a few days off to attend a presentation and discussion of recent advances in their special fields, or new applications in their changing world of certain theoretical instruction which they have already received in their usual period of training. Between these two extremes are a countless number of variations of desires and needs on the part of adults which should be met by those responsible for directing adult education. These needs and responsibilities are especially numerous and urgent in urban areas. In the development of Catholic adult education during the last decade, great progress has been made in this middle area with a slight step downward toward the lower extreme but with an almost complete disregard for the uppermost group, where obviously education is most appropriate for adults, as we have defined it for institutions of higher education. Our non-Catholic institutions, especially the complex state universities, stress programs of study for the professional groups and for their own alumni, sometimes under the term "continuation education," always with careful organization and administration. In fact, they find this activity of great value in keeping the alumni interested in their alma mater and in making influential and beneficial friends for the institution. Catholic colleges and universities would do well to take adult education seriously, and to make it an integral part of the academic family, just as much as they do the work of any of the usual departments. Thus far we cannot say that any great progress has been made in this direction, and this represents a serious gap in the general scheme of Catholic Adult Education. Secular education, generally speaking, does not have this gap. Furthermore, Catholics lacking the opportunities they seek under Catholic auspices, enroll in classes under non-Catholic direction. All the dangers and risks, to which the layman's attention is called in secular education generally, exist to the same degree in adult education. Catholic educators, especially in the field of higher education, by neglecting adult education are failing to that extent to meet their proper responsibilities to the Church and the Catholic public.

CHAPTER TWENTY-TWO

FINANCING THE EDUCATION
OF STUDENTS IN CATHOLIC SCHOOLS

About forty or a little more years ago the Abbot of the Abbey of Fort Augustus, Scotland, was visiting the United States in the process of establishing the Abbey of Saint Anselm here in Washington. I had been at The Catholic University of America for only several months and had much to learn about Catholic education, its aims and its nature. It was my good fortune at the time to be invited out to dinner with the Abbot by a mutual friend. During the course of our conversation the question of gov-

[1] The material in this section is drawn to a large extent from text of a statement delivered on the Senate floor by Senator Abraham Ribicoff (Democratic) of Connecticut.

ernment support of private education arose. My friend and I were rather smug with the idea prevailing in Catholic circles at the time, that we Cathlics did not want supporting funds from the government since we would in all probability lose our freedom and independence by accepting them. The Abbot, however, was insistent that we would one day want it and claim it as our right, since it would be impossible for American Catholics to continue to develop and support their own system of education while at the same time contributing to the support of public education. His statement was almost in the nature of a prediction.

The question of financing the education of students in private schools has now reached a point where it has been called by responsible persons a deep controversy throughout this land which imperils the future of our nation. Certainly, it is necessary that every possible effort be made to solve it, but it will not be solved by either or both of the extremist groups. Unfortunately, the proponents of the extremes, those who wish the federal government to finance private education just as it does public education and those who want private education to receive no financial assistance at all have dominated public debate, in fact, so much so that the people at large are scarcely aware that any other points of view exist.

I do not wish to enter into any detailed discussion of this controversy but only to present some of the difficulties involved, and finally to present some suggestions offered by a competent person for its solution.

The number of students in private schools number in the several millions, most of whom are in church-related institutions. Certainly the education of these children and young adults cannot be ignored.

It is a fact, however, that religious teaching does occur in church-related schools. This involves the problem of the separation of Church and State, which principle essentially all Americans support. But there is agreement on both the fact that the Constitution does place outright limits on the use of public funds for private education and that within these limits some forms of public assistance are possible. For example, we may cite the National Defense Education Act, the college housing program, and a variety of grants for research.

The proponents of both extremes agree that public funds should not be used to support religious teaching. This is evident from the proposals made especially by the advocates of federal aid to private religious schools. They seek aid for the non-religious aspects of private education.

Although there are some who believe that there should be no aid of any kind to private education, the vast majority of the American people will accept some forms of aid to church-related schools, if nothing else than school lunch programs, teacher training programs, funds to promote the teaching of mathematics, science, and foreign languages, graduate fellowships, and loans for college students at various universities throughout the country. There is widespread agreement that these and other programs which aid students in private and church-related educational institutions are desirable and should be continued.

Probably the most difficult problems in this entire question of federal aid to private schools are to determine just what is meant by religious teaching. This problem has been more confounded by the introduction of the term "integrated education." The directed teaching of religion or theology for its own sake is religious teaching. There is no question about that, but when someone is teaching biology and presents the theory of evolution strictly as a theory, not yet proven to be a fact, he is not teaching religion anymore than someone else who would insist that it was a fact and that there is no God. Admittedly some would be willing to permit the latter but not the former. On what basis it is difficult to determine. Apparently, it is the common situation where the athesist feels that he has the right to express a negative view on the existence of God on every possible occasion but objects strongly to anyone speaking in support of the affirmative. It never occurs to him that he himself in his negative stand is after all promulgating and supporting a kind of religious view. Again, if when teaching history, someone, obsessed with the importance of integrating his subject matter, should conceal facts which seemed to go counter to his own views, he would be guilty of presenting very poor history but not of religious teaching.

Of course, if a teacher of whatever subject lugs in his personal views on religion by the ears, he is guilty of teaching religion. Moreover, this is not integration regardless of what so many think. As a matter of fact the occasions for a teacher to advert to some religious teaching in any subject except theology and perhaps philosophy are very rare. They arise almost entirely in answer to a question raised by a student. The teacher is then duty-bound to answer the student as best he can. If he wishes to place quotation marks around his answer, he may. He may, also, if he wishes, refer the student to a person, who in his opinion is better qualified than himself for the answer, or for greater amplification. But this last is not desirable, because the student will in all likelihood lose interest in his problem over night. There is no question whatsoever here of the teacher brain-washing the student with his own ideas.

In any case, it is high time that reasonable and high-minded Americans, to whichever side they lean, get together and work out a plan for aid to all American youth, which will be agreeable to the majority of the American people. By all means, let not any discussion of integration in Catholic schools be dragged in as a red herring.

The following suggestions made by Senator Abraham Ribicoff provide a basis for the solution of this religious controversy:

"1. Income Tax Deductions for College and Private School Expenses.

"Parents who pay the costs of a college education for their children deserve some help in meeting this heavy financial burden. They should receive a substantial tax deduction whether their children attend a public or private college.

"I also believe that income tax deductions should be allowed for at least a portion of private school tuition at elementary and secondary levels, and I am today introducing legislation for that purpose.

"Parents who send their children to private schools face a serious financial situation. These parents pay taxes to support the public schools of their communities. They also pay private school tuition. Of course the choice to send their children to private school is their own, and no one suggests that the public school underwrite the added costs which these parents have chosen to bear.

"Neither should we ignore the substantial saving to the public resulting from the fact that more than six million children are not being educated at public expense.

"The simplest way to recognize some part of this public saving is to allow parents a reduction from their income tax payments for a portion of private school tuition. These parents will still be assuming added burdens for having exercised their right to send their children to private schools. But these deductions would recognize at least a part of the burden that private school parents are lifting from the shoulders of all the taxpayers of their communities.

❊   ❊   ❊

2. Public Financing of Shared Time.

"The proposal for shared time is not a new idea. It has been tried successfully in many communities throughout the nation. It simply means that children who go to private schools might be able to use some of the facilities—the classrooms, the vocational shops, the gyms, the auditoriums—of the public schools in the community.

"A high school boy who did not plan to go on to college but who wanted to study mechanical drawing, for instance, might go to private school in the morning and vocational high school in the afternoon. Or a group of private school children without a big modern auditorium could use the local junior high auditorium for their school play.

"What I propose is to provide public financing of the shared time approach, especially as a part of any program of general aid to public elementary and secondary schools.

"The general aid proposals now pending in Congress provide for an allotment of funds based on the population of each state. I suggest that the allotment be based on the number of public school pupils plus an additional allotment at one-half the rate for public school students for each private school student who attends public schools on a shared time basis.

* * *

"A combination of these proposals—tax deductions and shared time—can help resolve the religious controversy in education.

"There seems to me no question that both of these proposals are constitutional and sound public policy. We now allow income tax deductions for charitable donations made directly to churches. These donations support not only church-related schools but also the full range of religious activities of the church that receives them. Tax deductions for part of the education expenses at private and church-related schools stand on at least as strong a footing.

"As to the financing of shared time, the payment is made to public school authorities for education of students who attend public schools on a part-time basis. This is plainly constitutional and sound policy as well.

* * *

3. Assistance for Special Purposes.

"In elementary and secondary schools, there is a wide range of permissible aid in selective areas such as mathematics, science, and foreign language teaching.

"An important national purpose is being served and religious implications are non-existent or at least negligible. We now use public funds for equipment to teach public and private students these subjects.

* * *

4. Teacher Training Programs.

"Students and schools are important, to be sure. But what is as important in the whole educational picture as our teachers? There are a variety of ways in which we can do more to train the men and women who teach all the students in all our schools —to improve their skills and add new dimensions to their knowledge.

"We now provide summer institutes for teachers of mathematics, science, and foreign languages and for those in guidance and counseling. These institutes are for men and women from both public and private schools. Why not broaden the range of these institutes? Why not provide scholarships for a year of advanced study? There is no reason why not. And unnumbered reasons why the talents and skills of all our teachers should be enriched.

*   *   *

5. Higher Education.

"In the field of higher education, I am entirely satisfied that public funds may be used broadly without constitutional question.

"The whole history and tradition of higher education differ significantly from schooling at the elementary and secondary level. The differences have been raised by a score of statutes passed over the years that have made millions of dollars available throughout the entire field of higher education.

*   *   *

"At a minimum these five proposals can provide a basis for a new discussion of the religious controversy. But it must be a discussion that looks constructively for answers, not critically for obstacles. We will not solve this problem if we stop our efforts because the Treasury Department says tax deductions for education expense are not sound tax policy or because the National Education Association says shared time is a can of worms."

In the interest of the welfare of Catholic Education in the United States as well as our country, let us hope and pray that properly minded persons will get together for a serious and constructive consideration of the religious controversy in national education.

CHAPTER TWENTY-THREE

THE FUTURE DEVELOPMENT
OF CATHOLIC HIGHER EDUCATION

As in so many features of American life, in this fast changing world adjustments must be made in the area of education, in Catholic education as well as in secular education. Because of its broader and more lofty goals this process will be more difficult in Catholic education.

After the second world-war several prominent Catholic educators caught in a common feeling that something was greatly wrong with a system of education which would produce men and women so lacking in patriotism as actually to obstruct the emergency efforts of the national government to conserve all possible resources for the war effort, strongly urged a return to the traditional program of liberal arts with Greek and Latin as the central subjects of the curriculum. This, of course, would be a great mistake, even if it were possible. The program of general or liberal studies in higher education must be geared to the needs of the time. This does not mean that the aims of college or university training are any different now from what they were when higher studies first came into existence but the approach toward those ends must be restudied as American life itself changes.

Some of the difficulties which have raised serious problems in the field of higher education today are the following:

The cost of establishing and maintaining an institution of higher education is rising rapidly. The general increase in the cost of living makes it imperative that the salaries of the teaching faculty, which have always been quite inadequate, and the wages of the clerical and maintenance staffs, be raised correspondingly.

The demands of American society for much greater service for its young people means special accommodations and accompanying administrative personnel. A generation or more ago a well trained physician and perhaps an assistant were regarded as adequate to care for the physical and mental ailments of the average student body. Today the lack of the services of a psychiatrist would be properly considered as a notable weakness in any college. Similarly, a professionally trained guidance officer with a well staffed office and other adequate resources is a necessity for any institution that would consider itself as better than average. I have not mentioned the supplying of non-classroom activities, which might be classified under the phrase "social life," and is certainly a *sine qua non* for a modern institution of higher learning. All these services require specially trained professional staffs, whose demands in the way of salaries are usually greater than those of members of the teaching faculty.

The rapidly increasing student-body, which is fast outstripping the establishment of new institutions and the physical expansion of those already in existence, requires a corresponding increase of personnel of all kinds to take proper care of it. This in turn aggravates the problem of an ever increasing salary scale throughout the institution.

A so-called explosion in knowledge which is pushing back intellectual frontiers at a constantly increasing rate demands better and more recently trained members of the teaching staff in order to train today's students better to take their places in the modern world. This is especially true in the field of natural sciences and mathematics. Catholic institutions cannot afford to give apparent substance to the old charge that Catholic education is backward or slow to move forward in a knowledge and in the imparting of a knowledge of the sciences. This requires a retraining of old teachers in these subjects, and a broader and more intensive training of prospective teachers therein.

A growing complexity in our total structure which makes greater and greater demands for a constantly higher level of competence on the part of all members of our society places a greater responsibility to contemporary civilization upon our institutions of higher education. Again for religious communities especially this means a much greater expenditure of funds for a better training of its members and for the hiring of better trained personnel from the outside to carry on the new quality of teaching.

Most important of all, however, in the new role of Catholic education generally and probably more importantly on the higher level than elsewhere is the teaching of theology. For many years in the past any nun was regarded as ready to teach religion, as theology was usually called then, by reason of her training in the novitiate. This, of course, is nothing less than an absurdity. She must have just as well-planned and scientific a training to teach theology as she would need to teach English, probably more so by reason of the great need for training our students well to meet the complex problems of contemporary life after graduation. It is conceivable that priests who have been trained in our better theological seminaries (better from the viewpoint of academic standards), and who always had a genuine interest in the subject will be equipped to teach college courses in theology. But these also would profit greatly from graduate courses in the field not given directly for their priestly formation but for a thorough and scientific understanding of the subject for its own sake. As Cardinal Cushing[1] has said: ... "the apostolic endeavor of the priest himself must be the effective agent of action; he must never be satisfied with his present ecclesiastical learning but always eager to discover new spiritual and theological insights. Unless a priest's reading includes the body of recent writings in the sacred sciences he cannot expect to be an effective apostle to the people of his own generation." Here again, care and a greater expenditure of funds by the religious community as well as the individual will be necessary if we are to have properly trained teachers in this pivotal field of theology.

In recent years there has been much open talk to the effect that the priests and the religious (men and women) should devote themselves to the teaching of religion or theology which is more in keeping with their vocation and the members of the laity to teaching in other fields and to administration. This, of course, touches on the fallacy that teaching in

[1] "The Church and Public Opinion," p. 29.

general and administration in Catholic education is incompatible with the religious life. We tremble at the thought of the eventual result over a period of years, if priests and religious are confined to religion and theology, and the laity to other fields. My fear is, with due respect to all concerned, that we will be faced with a society that will be completely secular. We are faced with the proposition, which I have brought up in part before, that the best trained person for a job should be procured, but at the same time a rather even proportion of religious and lay is highly desirable, in fact, a necessity, if a so-called "Catholic atmosphere" is to prevail in our Catholic institutions. This phrase, "Catholic atmosphere" has been defined by the Reverend John R. Crowley, S.J., [1] as "the impact upon students of the Church's life fully and vibrantly lived."

Another idea with regard to the future development of Catholic education which gives some of us serious pause is that in view of the difficulties mentioned above some portion of the Catholic educational system should be entirely abandoned, and Catholics should concentrate on that portion of it which will bring about the more lasting and important results. In fact, some steps have already been taken in this direction. The great problem is: "Which portion of the system will be cut out?" If we take the lowest part, the grades, we are faced by

[1] The COMMONWEAL, 1963, p. 326.

the generally accepted admonition of professional psychologists that we are giving our children over to secular eduators in the most sensitive and formative years of their lives. If we eliminate the upper portion, that is, what is commonly called "general higher education," we have only to look at dire results in foreign lands where this plan has more or less been followed for generations. It is notoriously true that while those so trained have a superficial knowledge of their duties as Catholics, entirely too many of them fail utterly to understand the full meaning and efficacy of the church and her sacraments. Indeed this is true in the case of some in the United States who for one reason or another have followed a similar plan of training. Ignace Lepp has made a remark which is of interest in this connection. It reads as follows:

"I cannot imagine how I would have reacted, if I had known in those days such Christian intellectuals as Mounier, Maritain, Gilson, and Guardini. I would have been forced to recognize that, by their intellectual excellence and by their philosophical and historical erudition, they were the equals of my Marxist masters. I would undoubtedly have been even more surprised to learn that celebrated biologists, physicists, astronomers, and other scientists adhered to Christian beliefs and were faithful to the observance of religious practices which we contemptuously considered as mere pretense. But I learned of this only after my conversion. Believers, in the old countries of Christianity, have no idea how firmly shut off they are from the mental world of unbelievers. [1] "

In spite of the many difficulties involved, it is very questionable that the Catholic population working as a unit cannot carry on its educational system in its entirety. The people of the United States should be proud of having evolved its plan for the education of its youth. It is unique in the entire world, and has been in existence long enough so that its rich results are evident. Furthermore, it is by no means a foregone conclusion that no aid will ever be forthcoming for Catholic schools from the federal or state governments. It seems to me that it would be premature at this time to abandon any part of our school system for any apparent reason.

[1] *Atheism in Our Time*, trans. by Bernard Murchland, C.S.C., New York: Macmillan Co., 1963. p. 23.

CHAPTER TWENTY-FOUR

A FINAL APPRAISAL OF
CATHOLIC HIGHER EDUCATION

To give an honest and objective appraisal of Catholic higher education in the United States is indeed a difficult task. Such evaluations, however, have been made, but rarely, if ever, have they been made on worthy and acceptable principles. Too often they are made on such comparatively insignificant factors as enrollment, plant, and the accomplishment of alumni in the field of politics, the writing of Broadway hits and best-sellers, rather than on the productivity of the alumni in the field of influential thought. I do not mean to insinuate that the alumni of our Catholic colleges have produced nothing in the field of influential thought but

I am forced to admit that it is little, and, such as it is, is not recognized by our own critics. In an apparent effort to make out the best possible case for Catholic higher education emphasis is placed on extravertism.

First of all, higher education in our land must be divided into at least two main parts, each of which has aims and purposes quite different from the other, and so must be appraised differently. To complicate the situation still more, the two parts to which I refer sometimes overlap in their aims, and claim to do so with every right due an institution of its kind. It is assumed that this overlapping is quite proper and should surprise no one.

In the scale of higher education collegiate work, so-called, comes first chronologically in the life of a student, and is the easiest to define. It deals with undergraduate studies and, theoretically at least, prepares the student for graduate or university work. But the role of the college in our educational system has by the deliberate choice of college educators changed somewhat in many institutions recently.

Up until the turn of the century, the college was content to turn out gentlemen and gentlewomen prepared to meet the problems of life in a general way. They might well be prepared also to teach and even have had specialized training in one of the professions. But within the last generation or a little more the final two years of the college program have assumed the appearance of graduate work, an activity of the university, strictly speaking. A growing and rather extensive trend is to consider the first two years of a college program as background studies, a training in breadth, and the last two years as a period of specialization in a single field with some of its ancillary areas, a training in depth. These two parts of the college program are regularly referred to as the lower and the upper divisions. Some colleges have even extended their activities through a fifth year and in some instances have granted the Master's degree for this work, a prerogative ordinarily associated with the graduate school, which is usually considered the very back bone of the American university. It must be admitted, however, that certain college administrators, realizing that the work of a fifth year lacked a strictly university character, give a certificate rather than a graduate degree for the studies of this extra year. Furthermore, the professions: law, medicine, social work, and to some extent engineering have insisted that their students have the general training of the college before they enter upon the specialized instruction of the professions. Other professions such as nursing and usually engineering are attached to a so-called university group while keeping their entity and are thus able to draw on the general courses of the college to give breadth and culture to their undergraduate programs, to supplement their regular professional courses by participating in some of the courses of other graduate schools of the university. It is interesting to note that all this is a reversion to the traditional organization of the university as seen in Europe today. The first two years of American college work is carried on by the German gymnasium, the French lycée, and the Italian liceo. On completing this work, the student goes to the university where, roughly speaking, he will complete the work of the last two years of an American college as an integral part of his university studies.

The most difficult nut to crack, however, is to make some order out of the chaos of the organization of the American university. We have tried above to give as clear a description as possible of this problem. [1] All this has brought me to the conclusion that in making any evaluation of American Catholic higher education, I must extricate myself from the organizational confusion which it shares with all the rest of American higher education and base my appraisal on the instruction, undergraduate, graduate, or both, which the institutions involved actually offer rather than be influenced to any degree by their names such as college, university, or institute. In fact in some states of the Union it is so

---

[1] Cf. Chapter One, The Organization of Institutions of Higher Education.

easy to procure a charter or to be incorporated as an institution of higher education and to be empowered to grant every conceivable degree that some institutions bear the name of university which from the viewpoint of the nature and quality of their instruction are no more than junior colleges.

To clarify my point of view still more, a recent author of a work on Catholic higher education [2] in the course of his presentation apparently lumps undergraduate and graduate work together and comments on them as if they were one and the same. The quotations which he gives from prominent Catholic educators may usually be identified as having been made with reference either to college or graduate education but he does not distinguish them as such. To illustrate my point I shall present several quotations made by the author.

The first quotation is, I think, definitely pointed at the college. "Father William J. Dunne, S.J., a former college president who is now associate secretary for the College and University Department of the National Catholic Educational Association, pinpointed the problem at a July, 1961, convention in which he addressed representatives of Catholic institutions on 'University Relations Through the President's Eyes.' He raised the issue directly: 'In

[2] The college Campus, Edward Wakin, New York: The Macmillan Company, 1963. I take this as an example because it is the last which has come to my attention. There are a number of such works all bearing the same characteristics.

some of your university relations offices the question is being discussed with regard to the emphasis to be placed or not to be placed upon the religious nature of our colleges and universities.'

"At another point in his speech he said: 'We have been speaking of a certain perplexity over the national image of Catholic education. It is not altogether surprising then, to find in these times a kind of 'shying away' from the religious character of our college and universities. You can observe this in many brochures and publicity releases. There is an obvious 'playing down' of the religious side of our institutions. Whether this is done to enlarge the green pastures of the fund raisers or to broaden the field of student recruitment I do not know. Whatever the motives are, I simply say that it is bad. [1] "

Whether Father Dunne's charges are true or not is largely a matter of opinion. In any case I do not think that he has touched upon the matter of greatest concern in the Catholic college. This has to do with teaching. Entirely too many Catholics, including Catholics who should know better, believe that a college becomes Catholic in the best sense through its chapel, religious exercises, and general Catholic atmosphere. All this is an important factor, but it is only part of the matter. Little thought or knowledge is exhibited about what we know as integration in teaching. [1]

[1] Pp. 194-5.   [2] This has been described in Chapter Six above, The College Curriculum and the Importance of Integration.

While there has been some comment about this greatest weakness on the intellectual side, few critics, if any, have thoroughly analyzed the problem and attributed it to the lack of integrated teachers and teaching. This is the key to the Catholic character of a college, and the successful attainment of this characteristic is to my mind the most important problem of Catholic education in the future.

Father William F. Kelly, President of Marquette University is quoted as having said in a speech delivered in Washington, D. C.: "Personally I am angered by the disservice to Catholic higher education of many in our ranks during the past several decades. The disservice lies in this: that their focus is so fixed on one facet of higher education, namely what they call the production of 'intellectuals,' that there is never sufficient emphasis put on the heroic strides taken by Catholic higher education, particularly in the past thirty years," and later he says, "What I am saying is that there is quite a considerable volume of splendid college education being provided for the preponderance of American young people in institutions that are not primarily research institutes." I tend to agree with Father Kelly, speaking, as he does, of undergraduate or college work. If one believes, as I do strongly, in the reliability of the evaluations of colleges as carried out by the regional associations, and examines the list of approved institutions as published regularly by them, he will find a very large percentage of Catholic colleges, especially Catholic colleges for women, listed there. Considering the short period of time that our colleges have been in existence, the accomplishment of Catholic educators in this field may be regarded as highly successful. It does, however, have weaknesses to which serious attention must be directed, if we wish to bring the Catholic college to a truly respectable educational level. Certainly Catholics have no good reason to be complacent. We must not be lulled into a state of satisfaction with the present condition of the Catholic college. More attention must be given to developing college faculties which are interested and successful in research of high quality. The dichotomy which exists so markedly in Catholic college circles between teaching and research must be eliminated, if the proper intellectual atmosphere, which so many of the laity are demanding, is to be developed in our colleges. A better balance between the various elements that go to make up a good college, such as social activities, intercollegiate athletics, and so-called cultural performances, must be attained. Even more items could be mentioned but these are sufficient for mentioning here to make my point.

Our universities in the true sense of the term, as instigators and stimulators of genuine research, hardly go back before 1889. Furthermore, such institutions can be developed only with time, money, and good leadership. It is my strong belief that in spite of some obvious weaknesses, Catholic centers of graduate study have increased only slightly in numbers but markedly in the general quality of their work.

The following quotation, which marks the end of the recent work, The Catholic Campus, brings together Catholic graduate work, undergraduate studies, and even the activities of the Catholic junior colleges, and again makes generalizations about them all as a unit, with which except in so far as cooperation [1] (not consolidation), is concerned, I cannot agree. All education must be free to develop as its sponsors see fit. Any attempt to force it to go along a special path not supported by a strong demand of some kind is doomed to failure. The history of education shows this clearly. Furthermore, the periodic suggestions which are made in the press and public utterances, supposedly to improve Catholic higher education, exhibit for the most part, a woeful lack of experience on the authors' part and a very superficial knowledge of the nature of such studies. The advances made by our graduate schools in recent years have been almost as remarkable and extensive in quality as they have been with the colleges. If one will look at the report made in 1933 and 1934 by a joint committee of the Association of

[1] See Chapter Twenty, Cooperation in Catholic Institutions of Higher Education.

American Universities and of the American Council on Education, [1] and compare the picture presented there with the accomplishment of our graduate schools today, he can get a very vivid picture of the remarkable progress made. But much more research must be done and many more specialists in research must be produced if the impact of Catholic higher education on this highest level is to be felt. The greatest obstacle in the way of achieving all this is financial—money for salaries to attract the best specialists themselves and, in spite of what is sometimes said, there are Catholics available in this category, who have been trained in non-Catholic institutions; money also for scholarships and fellowships to persuade the best Catholic undergraduates to come to our graduate schools. Catholic graduate schools are woefully behind similar non-Catholic institutions in their inducements to prospective students. Some Catholic educators are very open in expressing their dislike to offering scholarships and fellowships to graduate students. They resent being placed in competition with other institutions in this respect. But they must face the fact. Procuring the most promising graduate students is a highly competitive matter, and becomes more so with the years. Generous forms of financial aid and highly trained research teachers are necessary to bring us the best of student

[1] Cf. Memoirs of The Catholic University of America, 1918-1960, Boston 1962, pp. 115-117.

material, and the most talented students together with worthy salaries are necessary to bring us outstanding faculty material. Incidentally, we hear a great deal about higher salaries for outstanding faculty members, but essentially nothing about higher paying fellowships for outstanding students.

Finally, all talk about "a national planning board for Catholic higher education" is nothing short of ridiculous. Higher education is not a big business operation. It might well profit by some of the methods of big business, but the life-giving principle of higher education is complete freedom to develop under the direction of good leaders free to make their own decisions and unhampered by ignorant interference. Mistakes will be made and much apparent waste of funds and time will occur, but such is the price that we all must pay for almost any kind of freedom of operation. Anything like a national planning board would create more confusion than uniform growth. In fact it would stunt the healthy progress of higher studies. I am confident that Catholic graduate schools will indeed grow and develop, and will increasingly become worthy representatives of Catholic culture and education, if they are left alone to advance under intelligent leadership.

GENERAL INDEX

A

academic freedom, 121 f.
academic standards, 115, 227
accounting, 195 ff.
accouterments of formal education, 244
accreditation, 18, 33, 154, f.; state and regional, 186 ff.
activities, extra-curricular, 35, 60 f., 108, 198 f.; athletics and sports, 218
acts of incorporation, 212
administration, 29 f., 102
administrators, 32; of Catholic colleges for women, 65 ff., 125
admissions, 35; requirements for, 193
adult education, 18, 218, 241 ff.; parochial, diocesan, academic, recreational, 243 ff.
adults, 241 ff.
affiliation, at The Catholic University of America, 14
aims, 35 f.
all-around girl, 116
alumni, 207, 247, 268 f.
amalgamation, 204 f.
America, 11, 185 n.
American Association of University Professors, 127 f.
American Catholic higher education, 271 ff.
American Catholics, 250
American Council on Education, 214, 228, 277
American education, 156
American educators, 157
American hierarchy, 212 f.
American life, 260
American public, 158
anarchists, 151
apostolate, effective, 138
Apostolic Delegate, 157
Aristotle, 38
art, 52, 218
assistance for special purposes, 257 ff.
Association of American Colleges, 122, 214
Association of American Universities, 14, 28, 214, 277

Association of American University Professors, 135
Association of Graduate Schools, 28
associations, regional, 15
athletic programs, 26
Augustine, Saint, 93, 94 n.
authority, 12
autonomy, 162

B

bachelor's degree, 100; program, 101, 222
balance (between various elements of a good college), 275
Bea, Cardinal, 143
Becker, Carl, 12
Bernard, Edmon D., 98 and n.
Berra, Yogi, 9
between training of religious teachers, 263 f.
board of trustees, 21, 119
books, use and purchase of, 131
British trade unions, 246
Bryn Mawr, 23
Bulletin of the Association of American Colleges, 185 n.
budget, of summer session, 225 f.
business corporations, 42, 114

C

Cambridge University, 246
campus life, 88
canon law, faculty of, 27
"Catholic atmosphere," 265
Catholic college for women, 10, 214, 219
Catholic colleges and universities, 121 f., 219
Catholic co-educational institutions, 68 f.
Catholic doctrine, 27
Catholic educational principles, 198
Catholic educators, 156, 160 f., 199 f., 248
Catholic Encyclopedia, 26

Catholic higher education, some problems of, 34; final appraisal of, 18, 28, 268 ff.; aims of, 30; future development of, 18, 33, 39 f., 43; 170, 260
Catholic junior college, 176 ff.
Catholic public, 248
Catholic university, 71 ff., 120
Catholic University of America, 14 ff., 25, 28, 249
Catholic University of America Affiliation Bulletin, 123 n., 245
Catholic woman, 67
Catholics and the junior college, 183 ff.
challenge, of the Catholic college for women today, 32, 63
characteristics of junior college, 181 ff.
charters, Papal, 27; 212
Charybdis, of superficialities, 88
Chautauqua assemblies, 221
chemistry, 97
Chicago, University of, 245
Christ, example and teaching of, 36
Christian character, 31; education, 36 f.
Christian intellectuals, 266
Church, 128 f., 158 f., 248
church-related schools, 251 f.
citizenship, good, 55
civilization, 170
Clark University, 25, 245
classical languages and literatures, 49
classrooms of a grade school, 246
clergy, 18, 32, 137 ff., 158, 246
conferences, 231
college, American, 82 ff., 271
college, general, 22, 23, 30, 44 f., 47, 50, 53, 60 ff., 100 f.
college, of arts and sciences, 21, 22, 30, 44 f., 47; of simple organization, 100 f.

279

placement policies and practices, 196
policies, 156
political influence, 210
Pope, 26; Pius XI, 35
postgraduate work, 102
prejudices, of race and creed, 54
preparing for classes, 130 f.
president, 21, 119
President's Commission, 177
private homes, 246
private philanthropy, 206 f.
problems of Catholic higher education, 32
professional fields, 21, 22, 30, 55 ff.; courses, 58
program, integrated, 58 ff.; of liberal arts, 171; new, 225
promotion, 128
pseudo-intellectual element, 132 ff.
psychological problems, 66 f.
psychology, 42, 113, 217
public education, 250
public financing of shared time, 255 ff.
public funds, 251
public opinion, 18, 150 ff.
publication, 217
purposes, 34 ff., 39 f., 108 f.

R

racial and national prejudice, 208 f.
"refresher" opportunities, 142 ff.
regional accrediting associations, 163
religious community, 107; college for women, 169 ff.
religious life, 171
religious teaching, 251
requirements, graduation, 35, 108
research, problem of in Catholic institutions of higher education, 32, 69 ff.; chemist, 57; research, 71 f.; pure research, 73 f.; applied research, 73 f., 78 f.; independent research, 103; freedom of, 124; specialists, 125 f., 168, 214 f.; postdoctoral, 217
resources, bibliographical, 217
responsibilities of the general college and professional education, 32, 44
retirement, 119

revelation, 52
Ribicoff, Senator Abraham, 248 n., 254 ff.
"rolling stones," 133

S

sabbatical leaves, 119 f., 128
Saint Anselm, Abbey of, 248
salaries, 128; regular and worthy, 135
Sapienti Consilio, Constitution of, 27
scholars, 128
scholarship, vigorous, 173
sciences, natural, 47, 49, 52, 97, 216; pure science, 245; 262
Scylla, of unrestrained pleasure, 88
secular educational advisers, 199
self-cultivation, 114
semester, regular or quarter, 222 f.
Semitic languages and literatures, 216
seminar, 231 ff.
seniors, 105
separation of Church and State, 251
session, summer, 18, 33
sisters, 18, 160 ff.
shared time, 256 ff.
Shields, Thomas Edward, 160
Sister Formation Conference, 161, 164, 169, 171, 203, 209, 214
Sister Teresa Aloyse, President of Immaculata College, Washington, D. C., 177 n.
Sisters College, 160
Slavic languages and literatures, 217
Smith-Hughes Act, 214
social work, 22; functions, 59; integration, 60; social life, 105, 116, 263; apostolate, 152; 270
socialists, 151
society, American, 53
State Department of Education, 164
Statement of Objectives of The Catholic University of America Chapter of the American Association of University Professors, 124
student, the "whole," 89
student government, 116 f., periodicals, 117
study, independent, 115

Suenens, Cardinal, 67, 138
summer session, 216 f., 221 ff.
supervision of education, 24
supporting funds from the government, 254
symposiums, 231
synthesis, 90, 93 f.

T

tax deductions, 255 ff.
teacher training programs, 257 ff.
teachers, bargain, 17, 32, 125, 132 ff., 215
teaching, 69 ff.; freedom of, 124 ff., 168; stimulating, 173, 196, 215 f.
technical school, 30; competence, 4
tenure, 121 f., 128
terminal programs in junior colleges, 180 ff.
theological seminaries, 264
theology, 23; faculty of, 27; Catholic, 31; 42, 46, 92 f., 113, 128, 152, 189, 263
Thomas, Saint, 38, 93, 94
traditional program, 261 f.
transfer programs in junior colleges, 188 ff.
Treasury Department, 258
trilogy, 16
Truman Committee, 179
truth, 90 f.

U

United States Commissioner of Education, 91
United States Education Mission to Japan, 157
United States of America, 15; welfare of, 125 f.
United States Office of Education, 213, 234
unity, 90, 93, 94 f.
universe, order of, 45
university, 23; European concept of, 25, 28; American, 270

V

values, intellectual and spiritual, 88 f.; social, 88
vocational plans, 41; education, 42, 90, 113

W

Wakin, Edward, 272 n.
workshop technique, 228 ff.
workshops, 18, 33, 228 ff.
World War II, 246

282

THE DAUGHTERS OF ST. PAUL

In Massachusetts
>50 St. Paul's Avenue
>Jamaica Plain,
>*Boston 30, Mass.*
>172 Tremont St.,
>*Boston 11, Mass.*
>381 Dorchester St.
>*So. Boston 27, Mass.*
>325 Main St.
>*Fitchburg, Mass.*

In New York
>78 Fort Place,
>*Staten Island 1, N.Y.*
>625 East 187th Street
>*Bronx, N.Y.*
>39 Erie St.,
>*Buffalo 2, N.Y.*

In Connecticut
>202 Fairfield Ave.,
>*Bridgeport, Conn.*

In Ohio
>141 West Rayen Ave.,
>*Youngstown 3, Ohio*
>*Cleveland, Ohio*

In Texas
>114 East Main Plaza,
>*San Antonio 5, Texas*

In California
>1570 Fifth Ave.,
>*San Diego 1, Calif.*

In Florida
>2700 Biscayne Blvd.
>*Miami 37, Florida*

In Louisiana
>86 Bolton Ave.,
>*Alexandria, La.*

In Canada
>8885 Blvd. Lacordaire,
>St. Leonard Deport-Maurice,
>*Montreal, Canada*
>1063 St. Clair Ave. West,
>*Toronto, Canada*

In England
>29 Beauchamp Place,
>*London, S.W. 3, England*

In India
>Water Field Road Extension,
>Plot N. 143,
>*Bandra, India*

In Philippine Islands
>No. 326 Lipa City,
>*Philippine Islands*

In Australia
>58 Abbotsford Rd.,
>*Homebush N.S.W., Australia*

377.8273
D31s

Date Due

60742

MR 26 '66				
MR 27 '67				
NO 7 '67				